Primary & Perfect

Primary & Perfect

Seasonal & Thematic Projects for K-2 Learners

written by
"The Bag Ladies"
Karen Simmons and Cindy Guinn

illustrated by
Cindy Guinn

Maupin House by
capstone
professional

Primary & Perfect

Illustrated by Cindy Guinn

Cover design by Keith Welsh

Layout by Candace Hollinger

Photography by Amy Oxner

Library of Congress Cataloging-in-Publication Data

Simmons, Karen.

Primary & perfect : seasonal & thematic projects for K-2 learners / written by Karen Simmons and Cindy Guinn ; illustrated by Cindy Guinn.

p. cm.

Includes index.

ISBN-13: 978-0-929895-62-8 (pbk.)

ISBN-10: 0-929895-62-2 (pbk.)

1. Education, Primary--Activity programs. I. Guinn, Cindy, 1959- II. Title. III. Title: Primary and perfect.

LB1537.S565 2007

372.13--dc22

2007031243

Also by the Bag Ladies:

A Bookbag of the Bag Ladies' Best

Math, Manipulatives, & Magic Wands

Bags, Boxes, Buttons, & Beyond

The Bag Ladies Videobag

Contact the Bag Ladies for workshops and conference appearances at www.bagladiesonline.com or bladies123@aol.com.

Maupin House publishes professional resources for K-12 educators. Contact us for tailored, in-school training or to schedule an author for a workshop or conference. Visit www.maupinhouse.com for free lesson plan downloads.

Maupin House Publishing, Inc. by Capstone Professional
1710 Roe Crest Drive
North Mankato, MN 56003

www.maupinhouse.com

800-524-0634
352-373-5546 (fax)

info@maupinhouse.com

Printed in the United States of America in Eau Claire, Wisconsin.
012014 007967

Dedication

To Maupin House Publishing for sticking with us and coming up with new ideas,
to Emily for being so easy to work with,
to Ann, who saved our lives more than once with her creativity and hard work,
and to Jen, Vicki, and Paula, our loyal baguettes.
We dedicate this book to all of you.

–KS and CG

Table of Contents

Introduction

Dear Educators,

It is so exciting to bring you, the primary teacher, our fourth book, ***Primary & Perfect***! The Bag Ladies have taught all grade levels and know that the primary teacher is special, so here is a special book created just for you! We are positive that you will love the teacher-friendly, step-by-step ideas we have included, along with the projects, writing suggestions, and organizational bag ideas.

We find ourselves in a different grade level every few years of teaching. One thing the Bag Ladies have agreed upon is that it is easier to go up than it is to go down in grade levels. When you go down to the primary grades, you forget many things—like where they grab you, when you find a child wrapped around your leg in a guided-reading circle, or that the slightest question can lead to disaster, like "How are you getting home today?" The second thing we have learned is that the primary-grade child loves to learn and have fun with hands-on activities. These activities help students at an early age learn to follow directions, use fine-motor skills, and apply skills in a creative project that they are proud to take home and demonstrate.

All of the projects you see in this book have been done with primary students, so we offer you a few first-hand tips to help you achieve your goals in the classroom. When making a project, have part of it already completed for your students. You can also use a buddy system in which older children come to your room once a month to work with your class. Keep the directions simple and short as students begin by watching you before they start creating themselves. As you show a step in making the project, tell students that they have to sit in a "listening position," watch you demonstrate slowly, and cannot begin the project until you say, "Now you!" We have found that this little trick helps students prevent those impulsive cutting mistakes while helping you complete the task without the pain of having to start over again.

In the next few pages, we will take you through the organization of this book and show you the methods we feel are easiest for you to present to your students. We try to answer the questions you may be asking as you go through the pages. Being teachers ourselves has allowed us to follow our own directions and ask many of those same questions while listening to and watching our own students react to the directions we give them. So, grab your scissors and glue sticks and here we go...but remember, don't begin until we say, "Now you!" Most of all, have fun with *Primary & Perfect*.

Now you!

Set-up and Use of This Book or How to Be a Bag Lady (or Bag Boy) in Your Own Classroom

Monthly format

We have divided the book into months starting with September and ending with May, with a bonus summer-survival section. We did this because the primary teacher, although taking a skills-based approach, can teach skills using a theme that motivates and appeals to students. This sets the tone for the room, helps you select which books students will read or have read to them, and allows you to organize your instruction and classroom around the theme for the month. The first week of the month can be spent creating the organizational bag, and the three projects that follow can each take up another week. Included writing suggestions and ideas for extending the themes throughout the month can be used when and how you see fit.

Organizational bag

Every month has its own organizational bag and suggestions for how to use this bag for that particular month. For example, in October, students make an Autumn & Discovery Bag. This bag is used to keep the discovery unit projects together and organized for each child. Students do not come to us organized, and bags are a great way to begin and end a unit in sequential order with all projects, drawings, and activities together for viewing and assessment. Students take pride in having their own creative packet or pouch, and during parent conferences you automatically have everything together for each student. These bags are geared somewhat toward the month in which they are presented but allow you some flexibility to adapt them to your own unique classroom.

How to use the bag and writing suggestions

We have suggested creative ways to extend the themes and use the bags throughout the month—from units of study to individual and group activities—as well as writing ideas to get primary students motivated and excited about expressing themselves through many different writing formats. We developed the writing ideas around the theme and suggest topics about the student, family, school, friends, travels, and more. In October, your students will write about a new discovery they have made. It can be real or imagined. Students can write one paragraph or many paragraphs; they can draw a picture with a sentence or copy a sentence from the board; they can fill in blanks with words or brainstorm with the teacher and copy the sentences. This part is up to you to decide what will work best with your class. Another writing suggestion in October is for the child to make a silhouette of herself (you will need an adult to trace the students' projected silhouette onto a piece of black paper taped to the board.). The student then writes clues about herself for classmates to use to guess whose mystery silhouette this is. The more clues, the better! These silhouettes can then be hung around the room and later put together as a big book. In October, the class is also asked to write a poem about autumn. What a great time to brainstorm fall words, give a mini-lesson on poetry rhyming or not rhyming, and show students how to illustrate around their poem with small, colorful drawings. It is a wonderful season of sights, sounds, and smells, and we ask students to use these sensory words in their poems.

Projects

Three hands-on projects follow each bag idea, making the skills come alive for students. These projects can "fit in the bag" for easy storage, extend the theme of the month, and allow students of all learning levels and abilities to apply skills. For example, in October, the students make a 3-D Tree. On that tree, they can attach leaves with vocabulary words, with different colors to explore the changing colors of fall, or with rhyming words to create a "po-e-tree."

Activity cards

Activity cards at the end of each month's section extend the project and the skills learned. For example, on the activity card for the February Workman's Fanny Pack, students are asked to draw pictures of tools they might need to do a certain job in the future or to cut out magazine pictures of people doing jobs. These pictures are then stored in their fanny packs. In this way, you and your students are given ways to incorporate a skill (such as career tools) or skills into the monthly projects. Make your own activity cards that meet the needs of your students and curriculum and you'll be on your way to being a Bag Lady or Bag Boy, too! Much more than that, you are motivating your students and yourself with creative teaching and learning of the standards.

September

Back-to-School Backpack

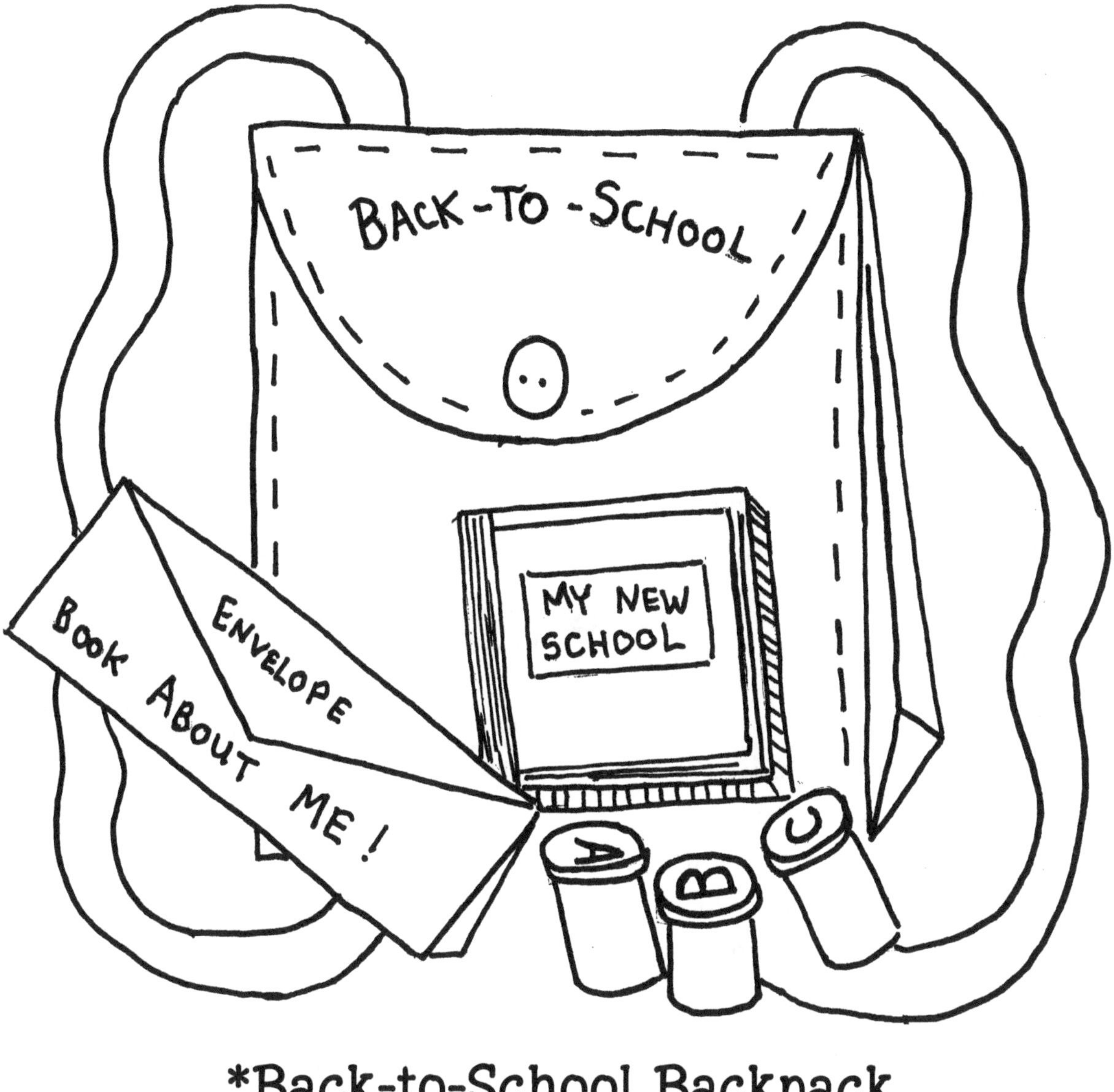

*Back-to-School Backpack
*Letter, Number, and Shape Stamps
*CD Case Journal
* Accordion Envelope Book about ME

Back-to-School Backpack

Materials needed:

*One medium-size brown bag

*Survey tape (3-4 ft.)

*Scissors

*Markers

*Crayons

*Rubber stamps

Suggestions for kindergarten teachers:

*Prepare the bags by drawing lines so the students know exactly where to cut.

*Working with small groups of students will allow them to be more involved.

Instructions:

(1) Lay out the brown paper bag as pictured.

(2) Fold down the top (opening of bag) to about 1 in. above the bottom flap.

(3) Open the bag to the original position.

(4) Cut away all of the top of the bag to the fold line except the back layer. This will create the flap of the backpack. Cut the edges so they are rounded.

(5) Fold the flap down and flip the bag over to the back side.

(6) Once the back is flipped over, draw four 1½-in. lines as shown in the diagram.

Diagrams:

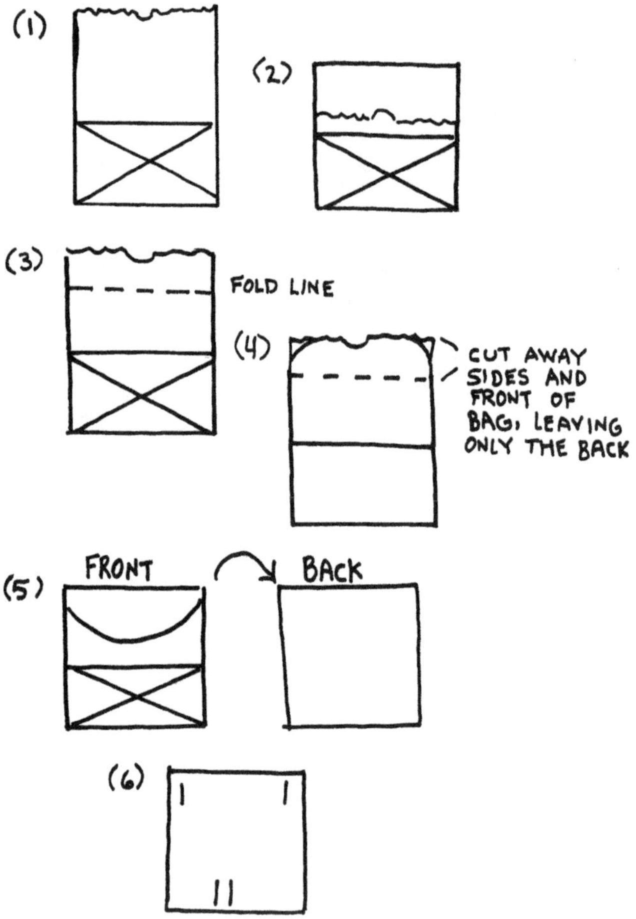

(7) Open up the bag, starting at the bottom of the bag, and string survey tape through the bottom slit first.

(8) Now string the survey tape through each side on the top of the bag, leaving the tape loose enough for your arms to go through the loops.

(9) Decorate the backpack with crayons, markers, and rubber stamps, and your backpack is ready to wear!

(7)

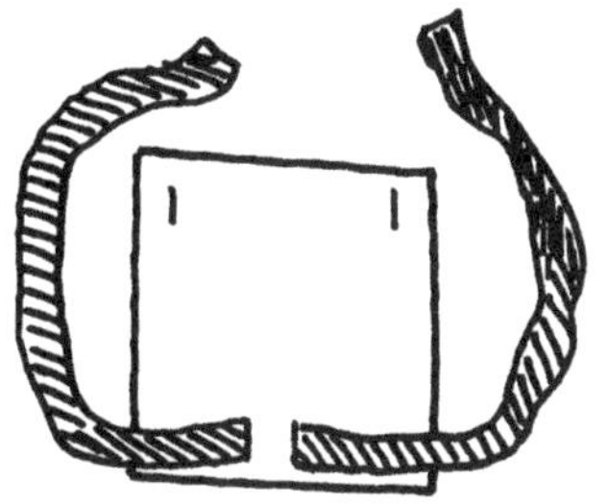

(8)

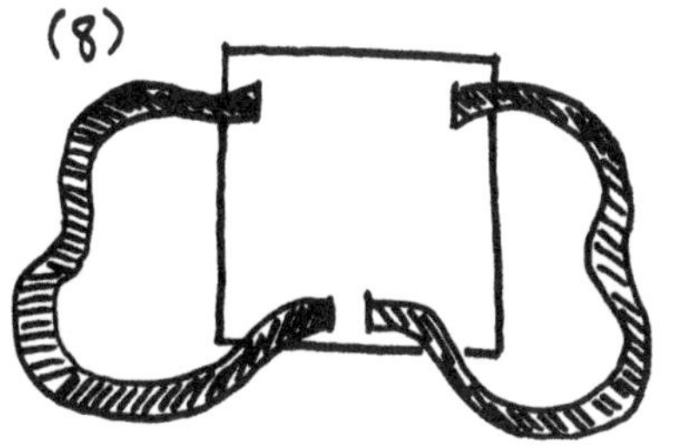

How to Use the Back-to-School Backpack

*Open House - Put all the important papers for Open House inside the backpack. Hang them on students' chairs, and parents will wear them home.

*Personal Collections - Students love to collect things. For show-and-tell, allow students to bring in a personal collection that fits into the backpack.

*Field Trips - When you take students on a field trip, they can use their backpacks to store the things they collected.

*Unit of Study - During a unit of study, allow students to store projects, notes, vocabulary words, and activity sheets in the backpacks. When the unit is over, allow them to take home all the materials in the backpack.

September Writing Suggestions

*Students can help you brainstorm words to match each letter of the alphabet. These words should relate to being in ______ grade. Assign each student a letter page to write, illustrate, and decorate. Turn it into a class book and allow students to take it home in their backpacks.

*Students can help you write a script for a video about their new grade and classroom. Create a video to show at Open House that will feature the students. The video can include a brief tour of the classroom, students introducing themselves, normal classroom activities, and routines.

*Students can write a letter to their parents for Open House. Then during Open House, provide time for parents to write a letter back to their child.

Letter, Number, and Shape Stamps

Materials needed:

*Fun FoamPre-cut, craft-foam numbers letters, or shapes

*Empty 35 mm film containers, one for each number, letter, or shape stamp

*Extra-strong glue

*Ink pads

*Paper

Instructions:

(1) Each film container will make one rubber stamp. Select one fun foam piece from the package.

(2) Using extra-strong glue, glue one foam shape to the lid of each film container.

Remember to glue them on backwards so they stamp correctly.

(3) Allow the glue to dry completely before you use these as rubber stamps.

(4) Once the glue is dry, your rubber stamps are ready to use. Gently touch the craft-foam shape to the ink pad and press it onto paper.

Suggestions for kindergarten teachers:

*You will probably want to collect the supplies and create these stamps for your students.

*Replace the ink pads with damp sponges soaked with tempera paint.

Diagrams:

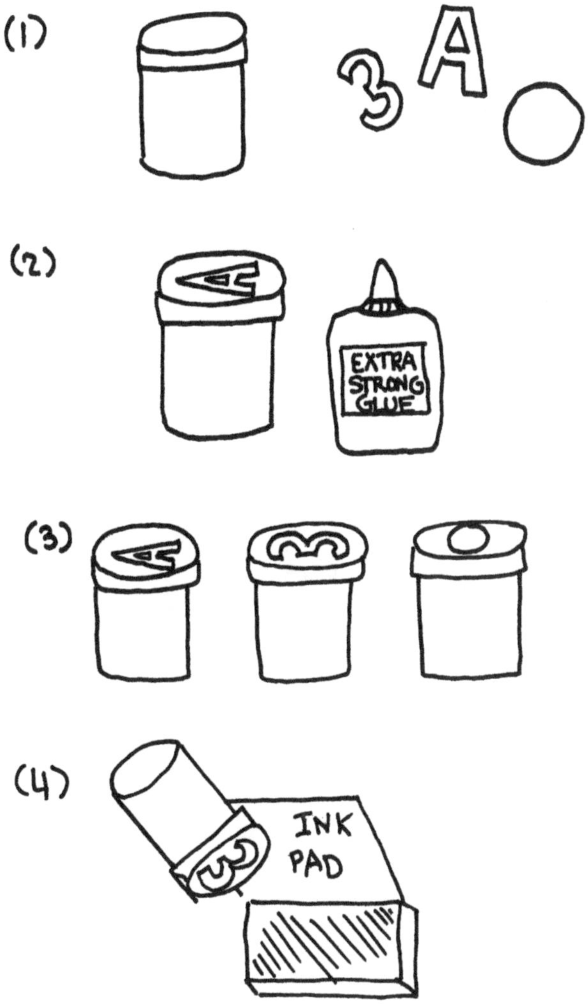

(5) Use your rubber stamps to create math problems, words, patterns, or designs.

(5)

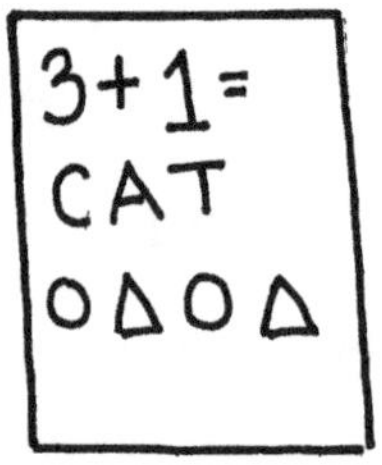

***Helpful hints** – You can substitute water-based markers for the ink pads. Just color the number on the bottom of the stamp with the marker and then press it onto paper. You also can substitute different kinds of containers for the 35 mm film containers. Any container with a large, flat lid or small blocks of wood will work to make the stamps.

CD Case Journal

Materials needed:

*Empty CD case

*8¼ in. x 4¼ in. white paper

*8½ in. x 4½ in. construction paper

*Crayons, markers, or colored pencils

*Long-armed stapler

Instructions:

(1) Carefully empty the CD case by popping out the cardboard or plastic insert.

(2) Place the 8½ in. x 4½ in. construction paper under the white paper and fold them in half horizontally.

(3) Staple the paper together on the horizontal fold line, then refold.

(4) Design a cover for your CD case journal that goes along with the topic of study.

Suggestions for kindergarten teachers:

*You should remove the plastic or cardboard inserts from the CD cases for students.

*Assist students with stapling the pages together or staple the pages for them.

Diagrams:

(1)

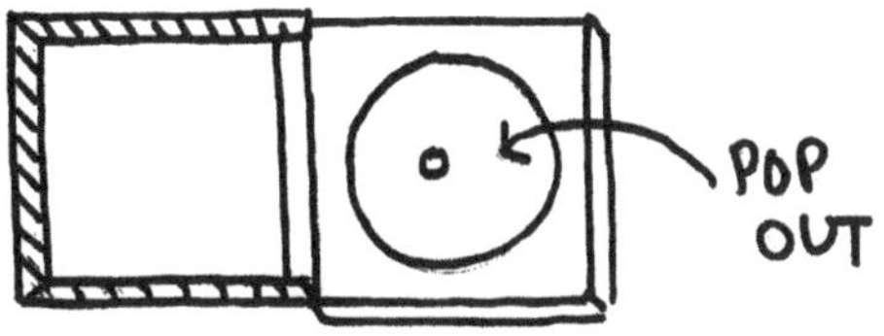

(2)

(3)

(4)

5) On each page of the inside, write your story or information from a unit of study. Illustrate and color.

(6) Place your journal inside the CD case for safe storage. A small pen or pencil can also be placed inside the case to use when writing in the journal.

***Helpful Hints –** Ask students to bring old CD cases from home. (Many people now store their CDs in CD wallets and have no use for the plastic cases.) You also can buy the cases in large quantities at wholesale clubs or office supply stores.

Accordion Envelope Book about ME

Materials needed:

*5 business-size, plain, white envelopes

*Glue stick

*Markers, crayons, or colored pencils

*3 in. x 5 in. index cards

Instructions:

(1) Open up one envelope flap and place it on the table where you are working.

(2) Rub glue on the flap part of the envelope.

(3) Take another envelope and place it on top of the flap. Glue together the flap and the area where the address is usually written.

(4) Repeat step 3 until all envelopes are attached to each other in a long strip.

(5) Using a marker, crayon, or colored pencil, label each envelope with a title. Examples: My Family, My House, My Friends, My Favorite Things, Interesting Facts about Me.

Suggestions for kindergarten teachers:

*Make these envelope books in small groups.

*Use peel-and-stick envelopes in place of a glue stick.

Diagrams:

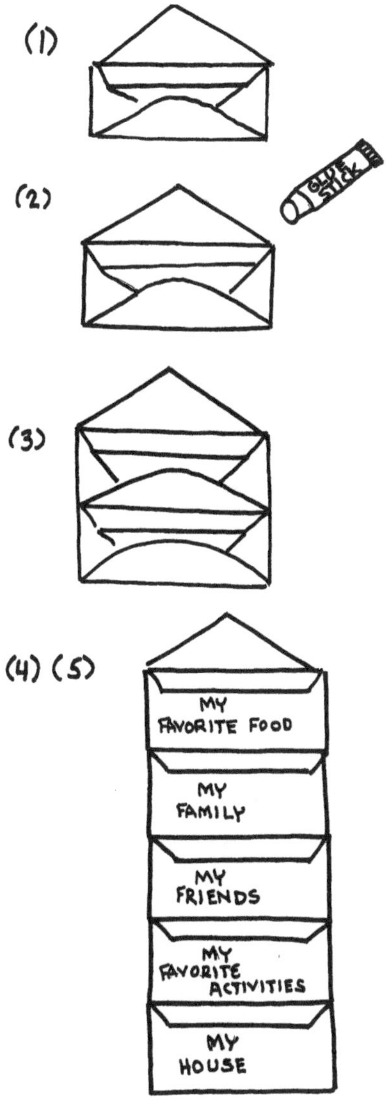

(6) Start with the bottom envelope and fold each envelope up on top of the envelope above it. Label the last envelope showing "All About Me."

(7) Students will use the index cards to draw pictures or write about each of the titles. This is a great home/school connection project that allows the family to get involved.

(6)

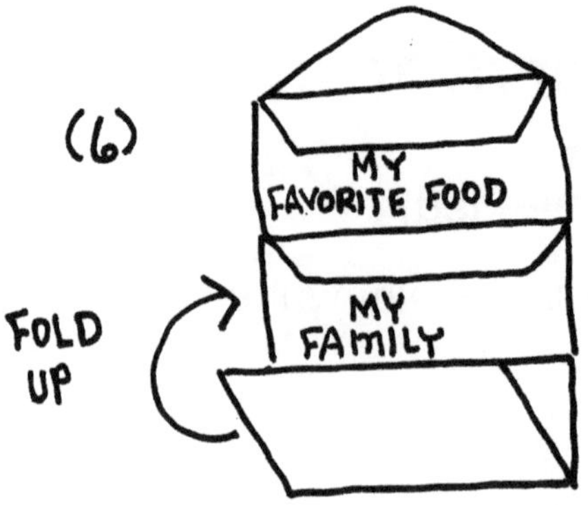

(7)

Activity Cards

Decorate Your Back-to-School Backpack

*Create a picture of yourself on your backpack.

*Try to fill the whole front of the bag with your picture.

Decorate Your Back-to-School Backpack

*Use rubber stamps to decorate your backpack.

*Spell your name.

*Create a math problem.

*Pick your favorite shapes to make a pattern.

Activity Cards

CD Case Journal

*Use the letter stamps to stamp each page in A-B-C order.

*Use the journal to write new words.

CD Case Journal

*Write a story about your new classroom, friends, and school.

*Share your story with your family and friends.

Activity Cards

Accordion Envelope Book about ME

*Label each envelope:

My Family
My House
My Friends
My Favorite Things
Interesting Facts

*Draw pictures to match each title.

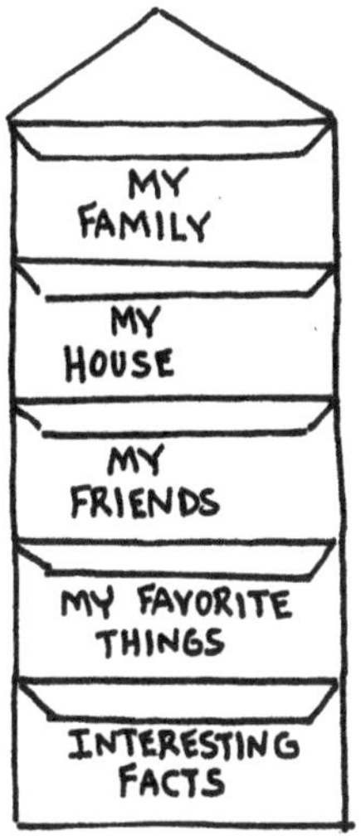

Accordion Envelope Book about ME

*Add more envelopes to your accordion envelope book. Think of new titles to go on each envelope:

My Pets
Favorite Sports
Favorite Foods

*Write about or draw each.

October

Autumn & Discovery Bag

*Autumn & Discovery Bag
*3-D Tree
*Discovery Day Hat
*Life-in-a-Tree Step Book

Autumn & Discovery Bag

Materials needed:

*Clear, wide packaging tape

*Brown paper grocery bag

*Scissors

*One 11 in. x 17 in. sheet of white paper

*Five 8½ in. x 11 in. sheets ofwhite paper

*Explorer Book Cover, Discovery Boat Pattern, and Autumn Tree blackline masters (pp. 150-152).

*Crayons, markers, or colored pencils

*Assorted tempera paint colors

*Five cotton swabs

Instructions:

(1) Lay the brown bag flap side up. Using the clear, wide packaging tape, tape closed each edge of the flap to create a pocket.

(2) Flip the bag to the plain side without the pocket and cut a pocket in the top using the Discovery Boat Pattern blackline master as your guide. Only cut through the front layer of the bag.

(3) Draw and color a tree trunk using the Autumn Tree blackline master below the pocket and add a background.*Stapler

Suggestions for kindergarten teachers:

*Cut out the pocket for the tree for students. That way, the tree will peak out of the bag correctly.

Diagrams:

(1) (2) (3)

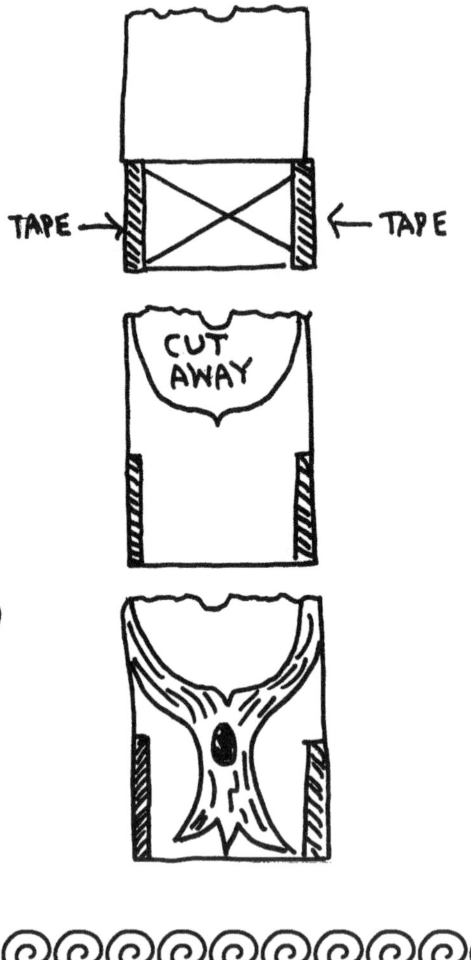

(4) Slip the 11 in. x 17 in. paper into the bag, and draw branches on the part that is showing. Next, add leaves by dabbing tempera paint on the paper with the cotton swabs.

(4)

(5) Flip the bag to the opposite side and trace the Discovery Boat Pattern blackline master on the pocket of the bag. Decorate it to look like a ship.

(5)

(6) Use the Explorer Book Cover blackline master as a book cover. Staple the blackline master to the sheets of 8½ in. x 11 in. paper to create a book. Draw and write about the ocean voyage and place the book into the pocket.

(6)

How to Use the Autumn & Discovery Bag

*Unit of study - As students learn about fall, plants, and leaves, all projects can be kept in their Autumn & Discovery Bag.

*Fall celebration - Invite parents to view students' activities and reports on Columbus, other explorers, and voyages, as well as a display of plants and leaf rubbings.

*Leaf collector - Use the bags to collect leaves. Tape leaves to paper and use books to identify the types of plants and leaves collected.

*Learn about pumpkins and scarecrows - Make pumpkins out of construction paper, cut holes in them, and insert student pictures for a classroom "pumpkin patch." Read books about pumpkins and scarecrows.

October Writing Suggestions

*Write about a new discovery you made or found. How does it help you at home or school? Write a news article and add a picture.

*Tell about your family. Use words in a list to describe each member. Are they funny or serious? Are they shy or outgoing? Make a bag puppet of one member of the family after you write about him or her.

*Write a poem about fall. Include descriptions about your senses: What do you smell, hear, feel, taste, and see?

*Make a silhouette of each student on black paper using the overhead. Each student will fill in a riddle about herself:

I have ____________ eyes and ____________ , ____________ hair.

3-D Tree

Materials needed:

*Brown paper lunch bag

*Scissors

*Glue or glue stick

*Small scraps of paper

Instructions:

(1) Open the brown paper lunch bag. Hold the bag from the open end and cut down all of the folded pleats to the first crease line to make strips.

(2) Continue cutting strips around the bag of approximately the same width. (Six cuts are good.)

(3) Hold the bag upside down so the strips are hanging down. Grab the bag below the flat base and twist, twist, twist to form a trunk.

(4) Students may enjoy giving the base of the tree a few "slaps" to keep it flat.

(5) Flip the bag over so the base is at the bottom. Take each strip and twist it individually and fairly tightly to form each branch. Be sure to twist the branches all the way to the end.

Suggestions for kindergarten teachers:

*Pre-cut the strips on the bag.

*Make sure you buy small, lunch-size bags. If the bags are too large, students will have difficulty building their tree.

Diagrams:

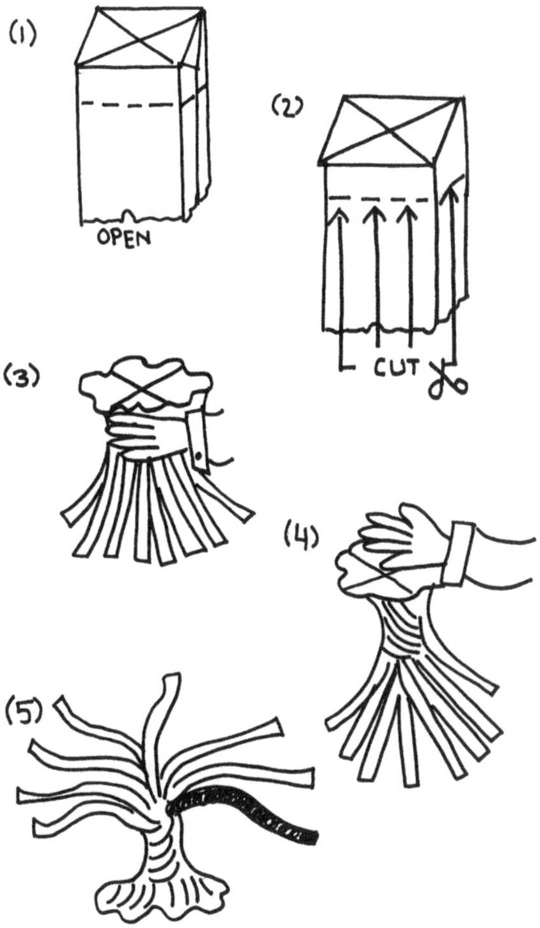

(6) For some variety, you can cut the end of the branch strips to form two smaller limbs.

(7) Students can attach information to the branches of the tree using the scraps of paper and glue.

Discovery Day Hat

Materials needed:

*1 brown paper lunch bag

*Scissors

*Glue

*Markers or crayons

*Discovery Day Hat Ship Pattern blackline master (p. 153)

Instructions:

(1) Cut the bottom flap of the brown paper lunch bag off as shown in diagram.

(2) Using the larger, flat part of the bag, cut it into two equal pieces in a wavy pattern. This will create two headbands. Decorate with a blue marker or crayon to look like waves.

(3) Cut out three ships from the blackline master. Use a marker or crayon to label them "Niña," "Pinta," and "Santa María."

(4) Glue the bottom of each ship around the wavy edge of the paper bag headband so the ships look like they are sailing on the ocean.

Suggestions for kindergarten teachers:

*Pre-cut the strips of the lunch bag and the wavy edge.

*Remember that one lunch bag will make two hats.

Diagrams:

(1)

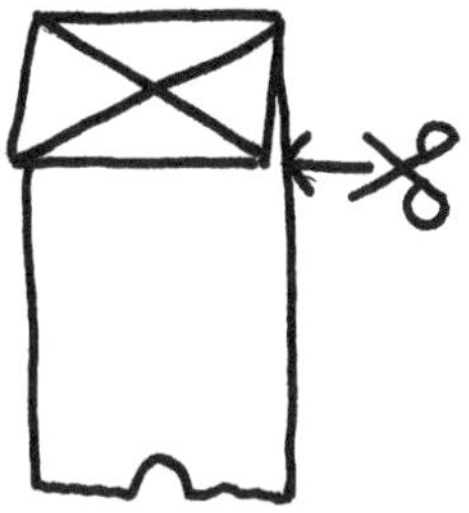

(2)

(3)

(4)

(5) The students can add words to the headband like "Happy Discovery Day," "Happy Columbus Day," or "In fourteen hundred and ninety-two, Columbus sailed the ocean blue..."

(6) If the headband needs to be adjusted for the student's head, use a larger bag or cut, adjust, and staple a bag into a smaller size.

(5) (6)

Life-in-a-Tree Step Book

Materials needed:

*Life-in-a-Tree Step Book 1-5 blackline masters (pp. 154-158)

*8½ in. x 11 in. copy paper in green, yellow, orange, red, and blue

*Crayons, markers, or colored pencils

*Scissors

*Glue sticks

*Stapler

Instructions:

(1) Copy each blackline master on a different colored sheet of paper (cut the master with two pictures in half and copy one picture on yellow paper and one on orange), and then cut out all blackline masters.

(2) Place the pages in order from the bottom to the top: near the tree on the bottom, in the trunk, in the branches, in the leaves, and then the cover page on top.

(3) Staple the pages across the top to create a step book.

Suggestions for kindergarten teachers:

*You may want to staple booklets together for the students.

*Instead of drawing the animals on each page, use clip-art animals that can be cut and pasted.

Diagrams:

(1)

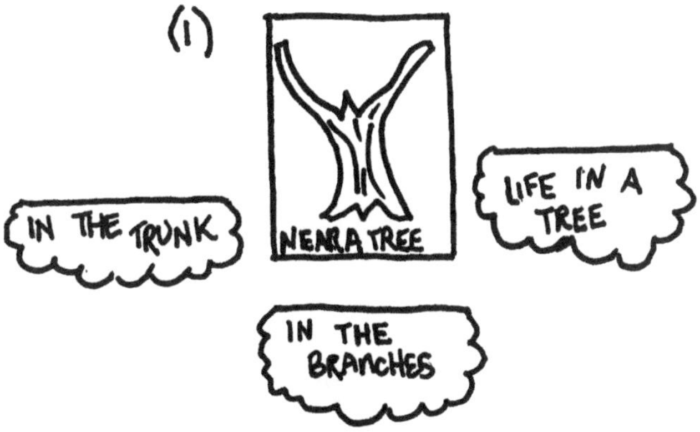

(2)

(3)

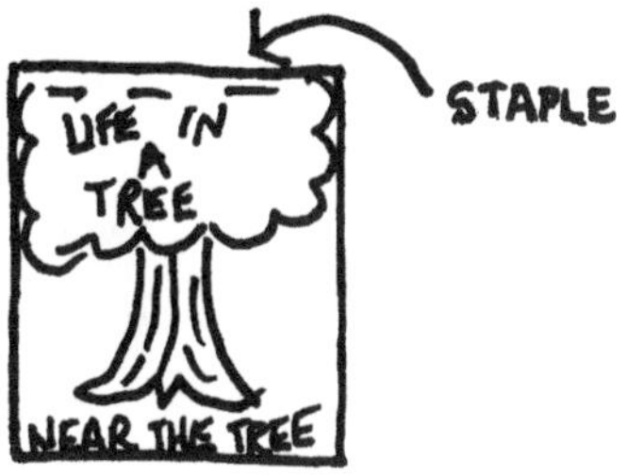

(4) On each page students can draw animals that live in each area of the tree:

Branches – bird nest, owl, squirrel

Trunk – woodpecker, insects, raccoon

Near the tree – mice, fox, cicada, earthworms

***Helpful hints –** Students can research other types of animals that live near, on, or under a tree and add them to their booklet. Teachers and students can also find clip-art animals for students to color, cut, and paste to their trees.

Activity Cards

3-D Tree

*Cut out leaves for your 3-D tree.

*On each leaf, draw a picture of a family member (mom, dad, sister, brother, etc.).

*Attach the leaves to your tree to make a family tree.

3-D Tree

*Make four 3-D trees, and decorate each one for a season of the year. Use cotton, colored paper, and tissue paper.

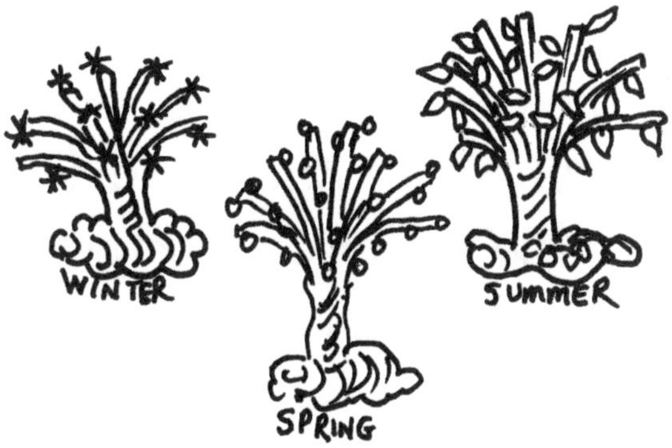

Activity Cards

Discovery Day Hat

*Write the names of Columbus's ships on each of the ships on your hat:

Niña

Pinta

Santa María

Discovery Day Hat

*Columbus sailed across the ocean to discover a new world. Add some fish in the water around your hat that Columbus might have seen.

Activity Cards

Life-in-a-Tree Step Book

*Can you think of other animals that live in, near, or under a tree? Add the animals you thought of to your Life-in-a-Tree Step Book.

Life-in-a-Tree Step Book

*Add details to your Life-in-a-Tree Step Book by drawing and coloring leaves, adding bark to the trunk, or making more branches.

*Share what you have learned with a friend.

November

Thanksgiving Bag

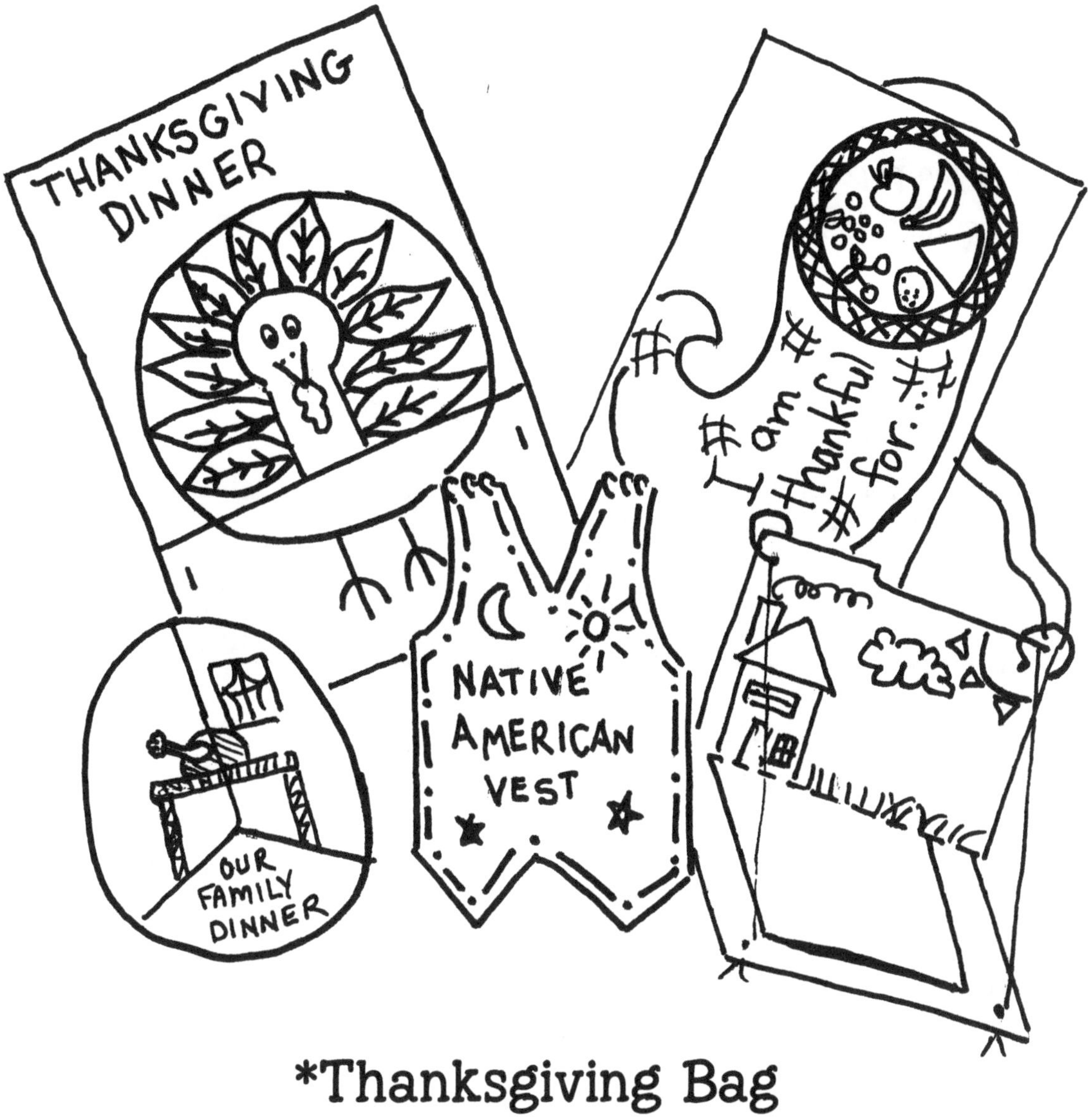

*Thanksgiving Bag
*Native-American Vest-Pocket Bag
*Paper Plate-o-Rama
*File-Folder Stage

Thanksgiving Bag

Materials needed:

*Brown paper grocery bag

*Two cheap paper plates

*One brass fastener

*Stapler

*3 in. x 6 in. sheet of brown construction paper

*Crayons, markers, or colored pencils

*Scissors

*Glue

*Thanksgiving Bag Turkey Head Pattern and Horn-of-Plenty Pattern blackline masters (pp. 159-160)

Instructions:

(1) Cut a window into the brown bag on the plain side near the opening of the bag as shown.

(2) Attach a paper plate near the opening edge of the brown bag by placing the plate inside the bag and fastening it with the brass fastener.

(3) Enlarge the horn-of-plenty blackline master and trace it onto the bag. Decorate it and add the words, "I am thankful for..." Turn and illustrate the plate.

Suggestions for kindergarten teachers:

*You may want to cut out the turkey heads for the students.

*You may also want to pre-cut the window on the paper bag.

*We usually have the students draw their own horn-of-plenty but we guide them step by step and provide examples.

Diagrams:

(1)

(2)

(3)

(4) Flip the bag to the side with the flap on the bottom. Staple the flap closed on each side to create a pocket.

(5) Trace and cut out the turkey head blackline master from the brown construction paper. Glue the turkey head to the flap of the bag and decorate to resemble a turkey.

(6) On one side of the plate draw and color turkey feathers to cover the entire plate. Flip the plate over and illustrate favorite Thanksgiving foods. Place the plate in the pocket when completed.

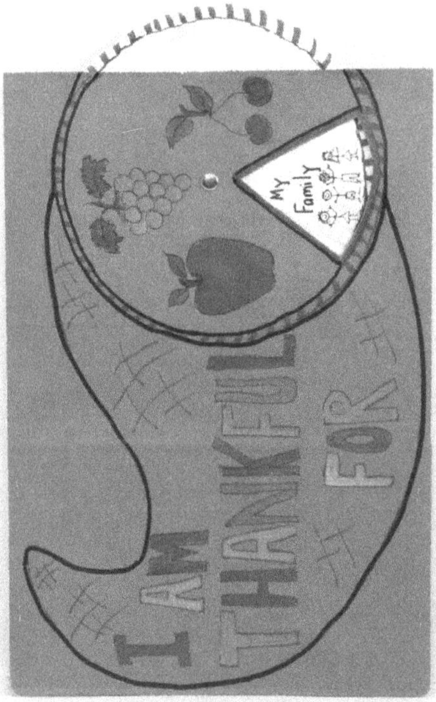

How to Use the Thanksgiving Bag

*Unit of study - Read books about Thanksgiving, the Mayflower, and Native Americans. Keep lists of books in the bag.

*Thanksgiving feast - Plan a Thanksgiving feast. Use the bag to hold all activities and plans for the feast and to clean cubbies and desks before vacation. Students can use their bags as placemats for their feasts at home.

*Discuss nutritional meals - Make multiple paper-plate meals, cutting foods from magazines or drawing healthy snacks on the plates. Keep these in the bag.

*Learn about turkeys - Make your own turkey and fill in a report about turkeys.

November Writing Suggestions

*Write about the people at your Thanksgiving dinner table. Tell about each member at the table and what is different or interesting about each one.

*Write about what you are thankful for and why.

*Tell a Native-American story. Fill in the blanks of a story with a small drawing that shows what the missing word would be.

*Write about your "favorites" and add a few details: favorite food, favorite book, favorite color, and favorite friend. Make it like a recipe book.

Native-American Vest-Pocket Bag

Materials needed:

*Brown paper lunch bag

*1 yard of yarn or string

*Hole puncher

*Scissors

*Crayons, markers, or colored pencils

Optional materials:

*Native-American Vest-Pocket Bag Pattern blackline master (p. 161)

Instructions:

(1) Open the brown paper lunch bag and cut away both side panels, leaving only the front, back, and bottom of the bag attached.

(2) Cut across one side of the bag bottom. Fold up the bag bottom and tape it to form a pocket.

(3) Place the other piece of the bag on top and cut a "V" to look like the neck of a vest. Then round the sides to look like armholes.

Suggestions for kindergarten teachers:

*You may want to pre-cut the lunch bags for this project and then allow the students to put the vest together and decorate it.

Diagrams:

(1)

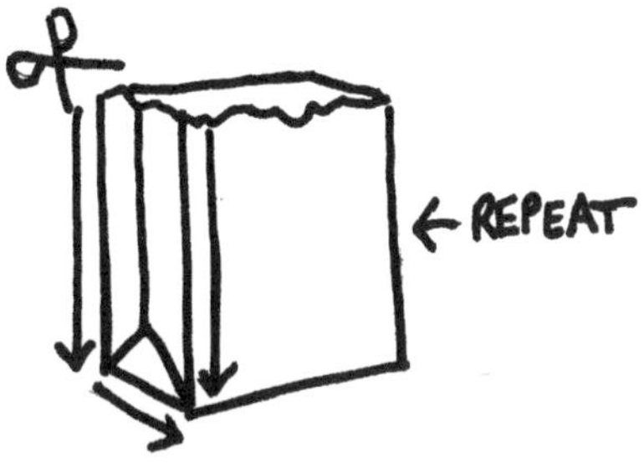

(2)

(3)

(4) Punch holes across the top of the bag at the shoulders, and then lace the front and back together with the yarn or string.

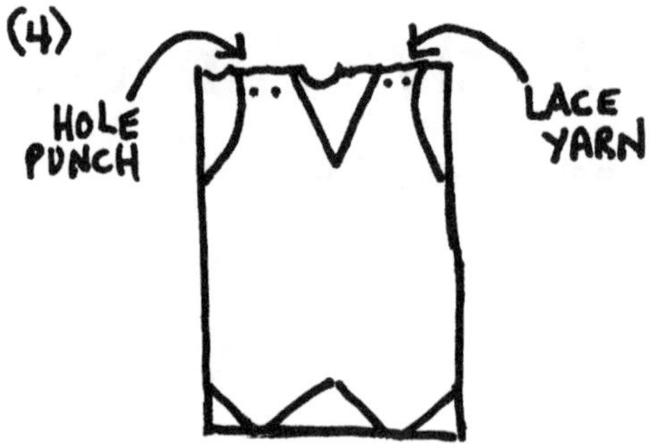

(5) Decorate the front and back of the vest to go with the unit's topic or trace the blackline master onto the bag. Students may store projects, notes, and reports inside the pocket. This vest can be placed inside the Thanksgiving bag.

(6) Students may want to add more pockets to the front and back of the vest by using library pockets or half of an envelope.

Paper Plate-o-Rama

Materials needed:

*Four cheap paper plates

*Construction-paper scraps

*One 1-inch square of sticky-back Velcro®

*Glue

*Tape or stapler

*Crayons, markers, or colored pencils

Instructions:

(1) Fold each paper plate in half. (We call this a "taco fold.")

(2) Fold each paper plate in half again. (We call this a "pizza fold.")

(3) Open the folded plates and cut one fold line to the center of the paper plate. Do this on all four paper plates.

(4) Draw an autumn background on the top half of each paper plate.

Suggestions for kindergarten teachers:

*You may want to fold and cut each paper plate for the students (steps 1-3).

*You may want to put the plates together for the students when they have completed all four.

Diagrams:

(1)

(2)

(3)

(4)

(5) Overlap the two bottom pieces of the paper plate and attach with the square of sticky-back Velcro®.

(6) Add stand-up characters or decorations.

(7) Tape or staple each paper plate together along the back side.

REMEMBER: Put them together in the proper order.

(5)

(6)

(7)

File-Folder Stage

Materials needed:

*One manila file folder

*Scissors

*Crayons, markers, or colored Pencils

*String, yarn, or twine

*1 yard of survey tape

*Computer-generated stick puppets

*Two pipe cleaners

Instructions:

(1) Cut a window approximately 8½ in. x 5½ in. from the front center of the file folder.

(2) On the inside of the folder, illustrate the background scene for your puppet show, which can be seen through the window.

(3) Hole-punch one hole on each side at the top of the illustration. Insert a pipe cleaner and twist it into a loop.

(4) Put the survey tape around your neck and place the file-folder stage in front of you. Slip the ends of the survey tape through each loop and tie the ends around each pipe cleaner.

Suggestions for kindergarten teachers:

*You may want to make a few file-folder stages and allow the students to create the puppets and backgrounds on paper.

*A page protector can be placed in the back of each folder so backgrounds can easily slide in and out.

Diagrams:

(1)

(2)

(3)

(5) Tie a piece of string from each hole at the bottom of the frame and again to the loop at the top. The puppet stage is now ready to be used.

(6) Use the computer to find clip-art characters that can be used in your puppet show. Cut closely around each figure and tape them to an ice-cream stick. The students can use Pilgrim and Native American characters or characters to represent their own family members at Thanksgiving.

(7) Your puppets and stage are now ready to be used to perform your story.

(4)

(5)

(6)

Activity Cards

Native-American Vest-Pocket Bag

*Decorate your vest pocket bag with symbols to represent things. Create a symbol for the sun, stars, animals, teepees, the moon, and others.

*Arrange your symbols so they tell a story.

Native-American Vest-Pocket Bag

*Write about and draw pictures of what you think the first Thanksgiving was like.

*Now think about your Thanksgiving with your family. Explain how the two are the same and different.

Activity Cards

Paper Plate-o-Rama

*Draw a background for the first Thanksgiving on one plate.

*Draw a background for Thanksgiving at your house on another plate.

*Add characters to each background picture.

Paper Plate-o-Rama

*Create backgrounds to show where the Native Americans lived and where the Pilgrims lived.

*Add characters for the Pilgrims and Native Americans.

*Write sentences about each picture and character.

Activity Cards

File-Folder Stage

*Create a background to show where you eat Thanksgiving dinner with your family.

*Create one character for each person you share your Thanksgiving dinner with, and use them to tell the story of your Thanksgiving.

File-Folder Stage

*Create a background for the first Thanksgiving. Remember the Pilgrims and Native Americans would have eaten their meal outside.

*Now, create characters to tell the story of the first Thanksgiving feast.

December

Animals-in-Winter Bag Book

*Animals-in-Winter Bag Book
*Bear-Bag Cave
*Birds-in-the-Snow Cup
*Animals-through-the-Page Book

Animals-in-Winter Bag Book

Materials needed:

*Brown paper grocery bag

*Two sheets of 9 in. x 12 in. construction paper (any color)

*6 in. of self-stick Velcro®

*Scraps of cardstock paper

*Stapler

*Colored duct tape (any color)

*Crayons or markers

*Animals-in-Winter Bag Book 1-5 blackline masters (pp. 162-166)

*Scissors

Instructions:

(1) Fold the paper bag in half horizontally and cut on the fold line.

(2) Using the bottom half of the bag, fold the top layer to cover the bottom layer of the flap. The top layer of this piece can now be cut to create a pop-up flap. (We used this piece to create a cave for animals that hibernate.)

(3) Using the back side of this same piece of the bag, cut a slit through the top layer of the bag big enough to fit a one-inch-long piece of cardstock.

Suggestions for kindergarten teachers:

*You will probably want to staple the bags together for the students and cut out the cave and slit.

*Guide the students through the creation of each page.

Diagrams:

(1)

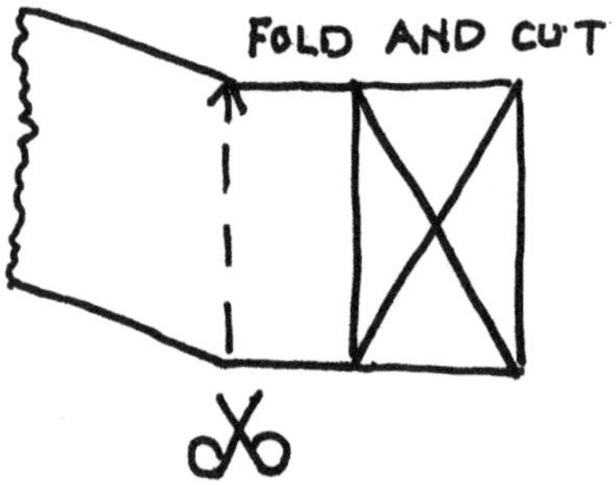

(2)

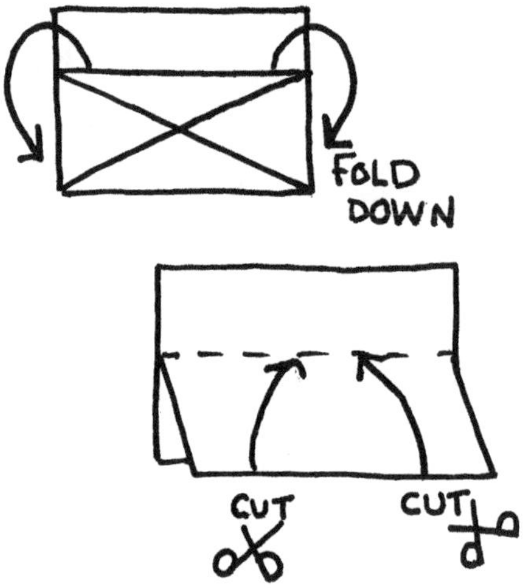

(3)

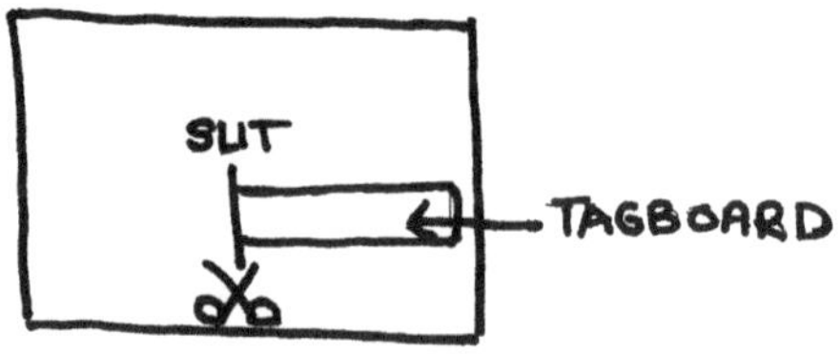

(4) Now lay the two pieces of the bag on top of each other. Place a piece of construction paper on the top and bottom of the bag pieces and staple along the edge to create a book cover.

(4)

(5) We chose to cover the staples with colored duct tape to create a bound edge. It also makes the staples more secure.

(5)

Creating the pages of the book:

Page 1 – Animals That Hibernate:

*Using cardstock pieces, create animals that hibernate and attach them with Velcro®. Decorate the background as a winter scene.

PG 1

Page 2 – Animals That Migrate:

*Using another piece of cardstock, create an animal that migrates in the winter. Glue it on and slide it into the slit. Decorate the background.

PG 2

Page 3 – Animals That Remain Active in Winter:

*Create cardstock animals that remain active all winter, attach them with Velcro®, and decorate the background.

PG 3

Page 4 – Animals That Sleep in Winter but Do Not Hibernate:

*Create cardstock animals that sleep in winter but do not hibernate, attach them with Velcro®, and decorate the background.

PG 4

How to Use the Animals-in-Winter Bag Book

*Animal studies – Students can choose an animal to learn more about. Bring books to class to make reports and drawings. Keep reports in the bag.

*Label names – Use Velcro® and labels to name all animals in the bag book. Add some others of your own.

*New environment/animal study – Add a new environment with all new animals. Use the bag book to include your new environment and new animals.

*Retell an animal story – Retell a favorite story from an animal reading book or design your own.

December Writing Suggestions

*Write about and/or draw a pet. Describe it and tell how to take care of it. What pet would make the best pet for your classroom? Draw the pet or find a picture of one. Why would it make the best pet for your class?

*What is your favorite time of year? Summer? Winter? Fall? Spring? Tell why it is your favorite time of year.

*You have just discovered a new animal. Describe it and tell where it lives, what it eats, who its enemies are, and what unusual features it has.

*If you had the choice of any one gift to receive, what would it be and why? What gift would you want to give someone else? Why?

Bear-Bag Cave

Materials needed:

*Large brown grocery bag

*Fiberfill

*Stapler

*White glue

*Scissors

*White paper

*Markers

Instructions:

(1) Cut about four inches off the top of the grocery bag.

(2) Cut an arched cave opening from one side of the bag.

(3) Fold the two sides of the bag together, and fold one inch of the edge over. Staple along the edge to hold the fold in place.

(4) Pop the bag open to form a cave for your teddy bear or other hibernating stuffed animals. Glue some fiberfill snow along the top of the cave and long the bottom opening.

(5) Make a sign for the cave that says, "Good night, Mr. or Mrs. ________! See you in the spring!" You might want to line the bottom of the cave with some dry leaves to make it comfy.

Suggestions for kindergarten teachers:

*You may want to complete steps 1 through 3 for students.

*Pick some children's stories that talk about hibernating animals to help students understand what it means.

Diagrams:

(1)

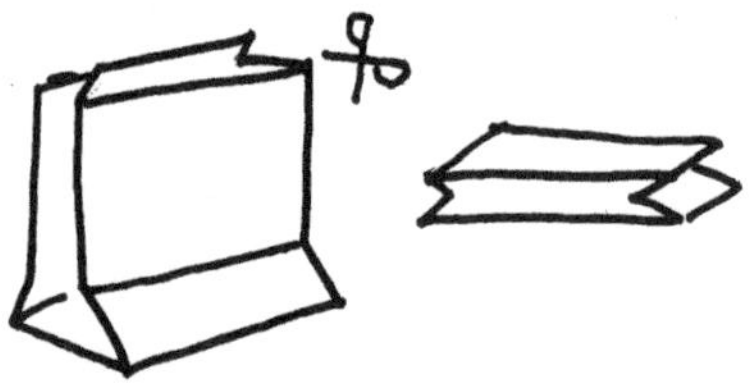

(2)

(3)

(4)

(5)

(6) Research and talk about different animals that hibernate in the winter. Remember that some animals that hibernate actually come out and wander around a little before going back to sleep.

(6)

Birds-in-the-Snow Cup

Materials needed:

*Clear plastic cup

*Styrofoam packing peanuts

*White glue

*Blue tempera paint and brush

*Twig small enough to fit cup

*2 wiggle eyes

*Scissors

*1 tablespoon of birdseed

*4 in. X 4 in. square of cardstock

*One small scrap each of blue and yellow paper

*Fiberfill

Instructions:

(1) Carefully slide one side of the twig through one end of the Styrofoam peanut. Tip the peanut up to look like a bird perched on a branch. Do this before you paint the bird in case you split the peanut and need to use another one. Secure the perched bird with glue.

(2) Paint the bird blue and allow it to dry.

(3) Cut wings for the bird from the blue paper and a beak from the yellow paper. Glue the wings on the back of the bird and the beak on the head. Glue two wiggle eyes above the beak.

Suggestions for kindergarten teachers:

*You may want to pre-cut the cardstock for the students.

*Once the students have created their winter scene, you may want to glue the cup to the cardstock. If you are doing the gluing, the quickest way is to use a hot-glue gun.

Diagrams:

(1)

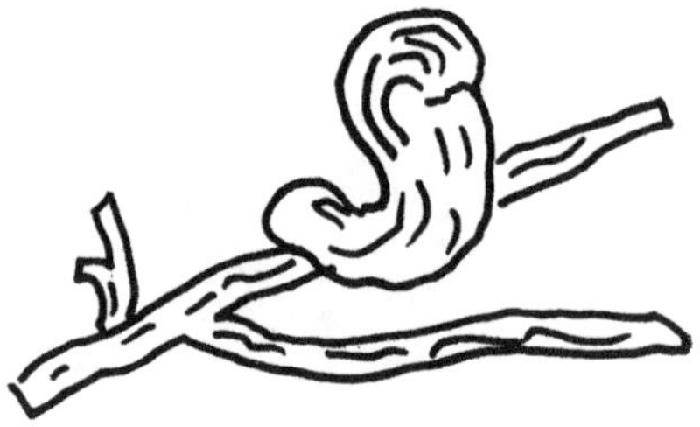

(2)

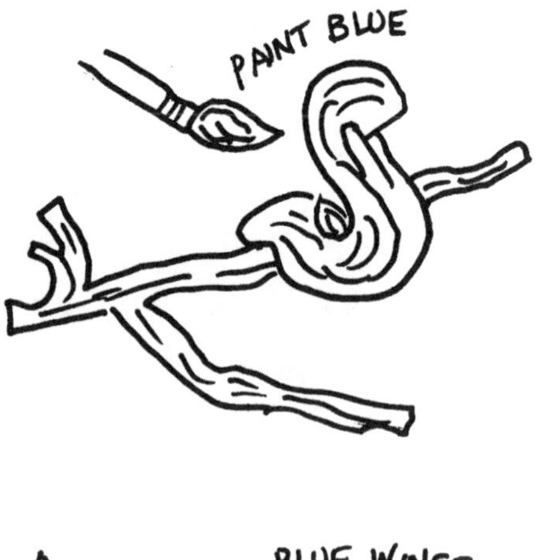

(3)

(4) Trace around the open end of the cup on the cardstock and cut out the traced circle.

(5) Glue the fiberfill to the circle for snow. Glue the branch with the bird on top of the snow and glue some birdseed in the snow.

(6) Cover the open rim of the cup with white glue. Attach the cup to the cardstock circle.

(7) Other birds and animals can be added to your winter scene. You can also create scenes for other seasons.

(4)

(5)

(6)

(7)

Animals-through-the-Page Book

Materials needed:

*11 in. x 17 in. white paper

*Scissors

*3 in. x 5 in. index card

*Crayons, markers, or colored pencils

Materials needed for individual project:

*Manila file folder

*Crayons, markers, or colored pencils

*Scissors

*Cellophane tape

*3 in. x 5 in. index card

*Popsicle stick

Instructions:

(1) The class or group should decide on an animal to travel through each page of the story.

(2) Write a story that allows for movement through different settings. Create the appropriate pictures to match.

(3) Draw your animal on the index card. (It helps to laminate your animal.)

Suggestions for kindergarten teachers:

*You will probably want to do the class project and not the individual file-folder project.

*Once the students have completed their animal, slit the pages for them.

Diagrams:

(1)

(2)

(3)

(4) Cut a slit in each page that is large enough for your animal to travel through each as you read the story.

Individual project instructions using a manila file folder:

(1) Open up the manila file folder and fold it in half vertically.

(2) Lay the file folder out vertically on the table with the opening along the bottom. Illustrate the top two-thirds of the folder and write a story on the bottom third.

(3) Refold the folder to the original fold and cut a line just above the writing, stopping one inch from either outside edge. Cut through only the illustrated side of the folder.

(4) Refold the book vertically and tape the ends closed with the cellophane tape.

(5) Draw your animal on the index card. (It helps to laminate your animal.) Attach the animal on a popsicle stick and slide it through the story.

(1)

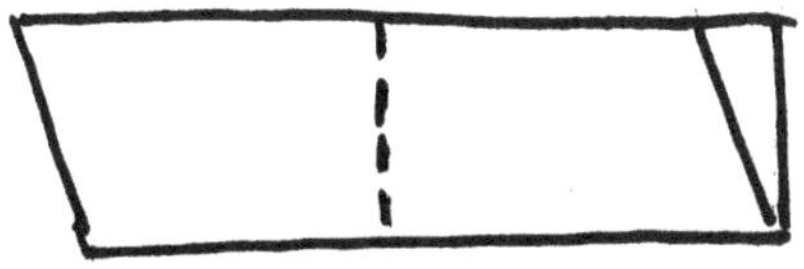

(2)

(3)

(4)

(5)

The rabbit lives
in the forest.

Activity Cards

Bear-Bag Cave

*Draw a picture of your bear or animal sleeping in its cave.

*Tell a story about your animal. What is it like to sleep in a cave all winter? How do animals feel when they wake up in the spring?

Bear-Bag Cave

*Can you think of other animals that sleep in caves?

*Draw pictures of those animals and write or tell a story about their winter. What are they dreaming about? What is the first thing they will eat when they wake up?

Activity Cards

Birds-in-the-Snow Cup

*Draw a picture of your Birds-in-the-Snow Cup.

*Write or tell a story about your bird. What is it's name? What do you feed it in the winter? Where does it live? Why doesn't it fly to where it is warm?

Birds-in-the-Snow Cup

*Draw another cup that shows your bird in the spring, summer, and fall. How will these cups look different? How will these cups look the same?

*What other animals could you feed in the winter time?

Activity Cards

Animals-through-the-Page Book

*Some animals stay active in the winter. Draw a background picture that shows this active wintertime.

*On a popsicle stick, create an animal character that is active all winter long. How would it stay warm? What kind of food would it eat? Where would it sleep? Does it have any predators?

Animals-through-the-Page Book

*Using the same animal character, draw a new background picture of a different season of the year.

*Tell about how the animal's life is different in that season than in winter. Would it eat different food? What food would it eat? Where would it sleep? Does it have any predators?

January

"I Have a Dream" Bag

*"I Have a Dream" Bag
*Coin Timeline
*Photograph-Pose Story
*My Special Dream

"I Have a Dream" Bag

Materials needed:

*Brown paper grocery bag

*Scissors

*Glue

*Ruler

*"I Have a Dream" Bag 1-4 blackline masters (pp. 167-170)

*Crayons, markers, or colored pencils

Instructions:

(1) Lay the bag down with the bottom-flap side up and cut down only the top layer of the brown bag (cutting a vertical slit down the center of the bag, stopping at the flap). Now, cut horizontally just above the flap to the edge of the bag.

(2) Flip the bag to the back side and use a marker and a ruler to draw a line down the center of the bag for the timeline.

(3) Use this line for a timeline. Cut out the pictures from the blackline masters and glue them in order to show the events in Dr. Martin Luther King's life.

Suggestions for kindergarten teachers:

*You may want to cut the slit in the brown paper grocery bag for the students.

Diagrams:

(1)

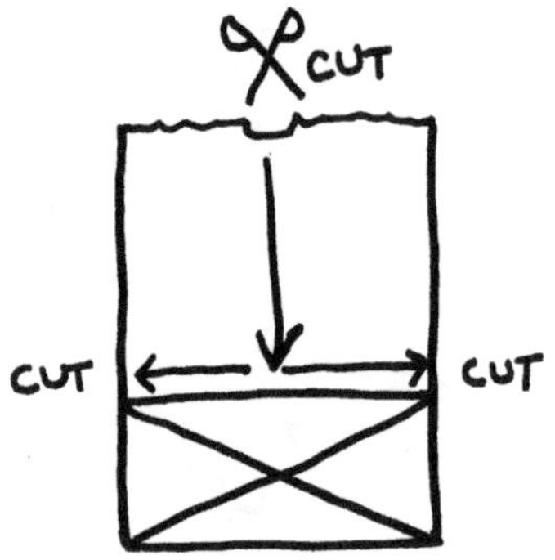

(2)

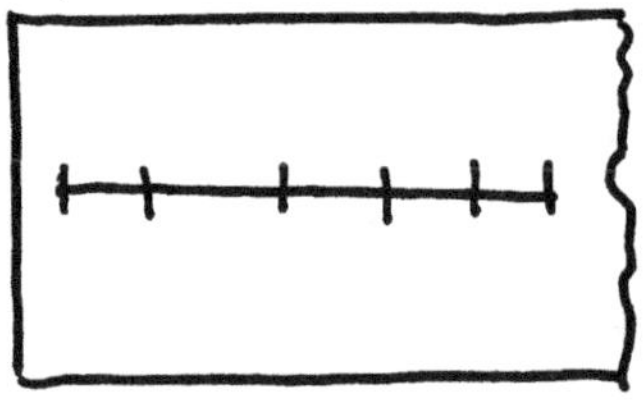

(3)

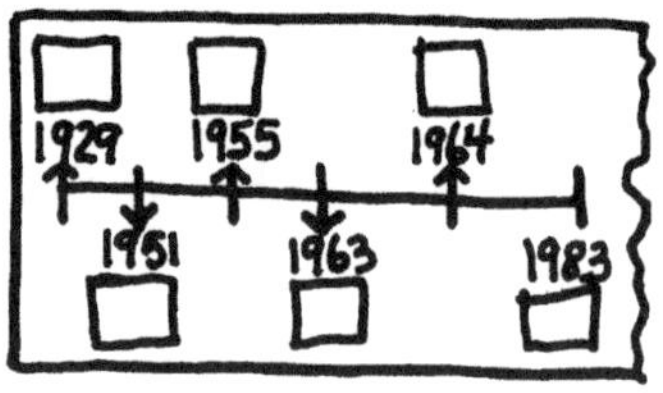

(4) Flip the bag to the other side with the flap, and glue a label and illustrations to the bottom of the flap. The label should relate to the topic of study. For example, this bag's label could be "The Life of Dr. Martin Luther King." You can use the illustrated "I Have a Dream" blackline master instead.

(4)

(5) On each of the cut flaps at the top of the bag, write a question about your topic of study. Then write an answer under each flap. Open the flaps to reveal the answers to the questions. For example: What was Martin L. King's dream for the future? What is your dream for the future?

(5)

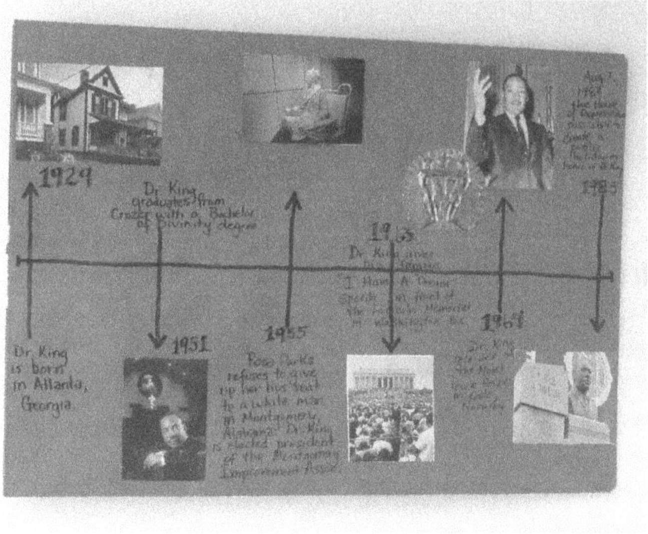

How to Use the "I Have a Dream" Bag

*Biographies - Students learn about other famous Americans and read biographies. Keep a list of people learned about and what they are known for/their achievements.

*Timelines of people - Keep timelines of famous people's lives.

*Timelines of events - Make a timeline of important school events. Attach them to the bag.

*Resolutions - Students write New Year's resolutions and keep them in the bag. Include goals for at home and at school.

January Writing Suggestions

*If you could change one thing about yourself, what would it be? Why?

*What would you want to be known for 20 years from now? Put yourself on a magazine cover. Use a photo or draw your face on the cover.

*Tell about your favorite place. It can be a city, park, tree house, anywhere. Be creative. Describe the place and tell why it is your favorite.

*Design the perfect school uniform. Tell about each part of the uniform and why it would be perfect for you to wear to school.

Coin Timeline

Materials needed:

*Coin Timeline blackline master – one copy for each year (p. 171)

*Coins with years matching each year on the timeline

*Scissors

*Clear tape or glue

*Crayons, markers, or colored pencils

Instructions:

(1) Begin by having the students search for coins with years matching each year on their timeline.

(2) Have the students fill in each year of their timeline with the year, their age during that year, a coin to represent that year, and at least three events that occurred in their lives during that year. Students can also include photographs or drawings on their timelines.

(3) Once all years of the timeline have been completed, cut apart each year and glue or tape them in order.

Suggestions for kindergarten teachers:

*You might want to have students draw pictures in place of writing on their timelines. Then help them write a few words individually.

Diagrams:

(1)

(2)

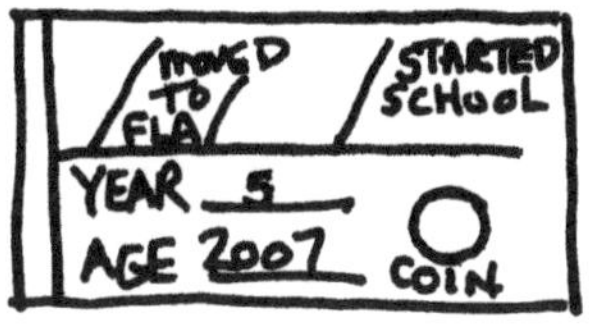

(3)

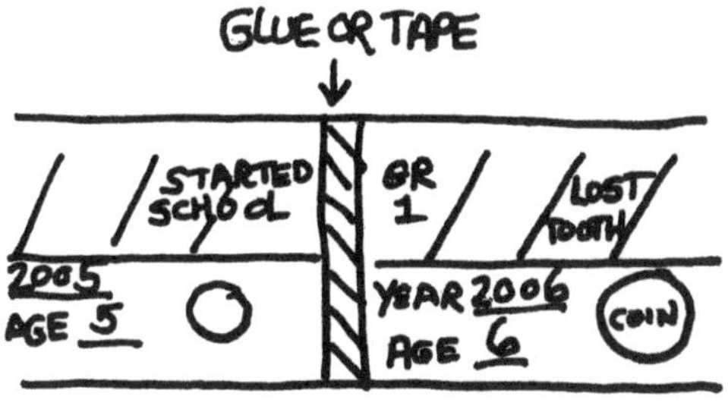

(4) Have the students share some of the major events on their timelines as an oral presentation or display them for others to read.

(5) The Coin Timelines can be stored in the students' "I Have a Dream" Bags. This activity can also be extended by having the students think about their future. Have them draw or paint a picture of how they might look in the future (10-20 years). Extend this by assigning a writing project in which students describe what they hope their lives will be like at that time.

(4)

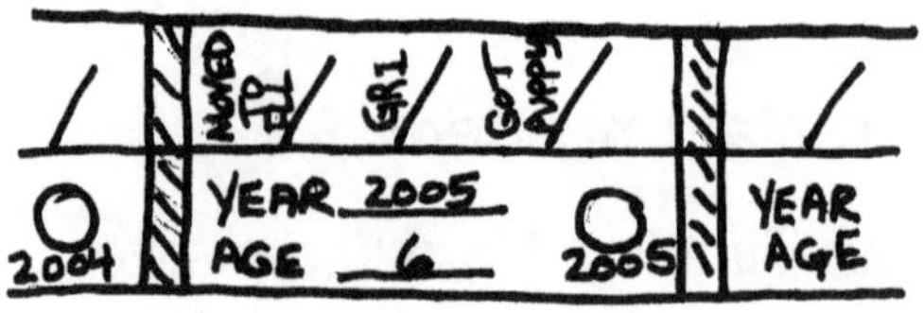

(5)

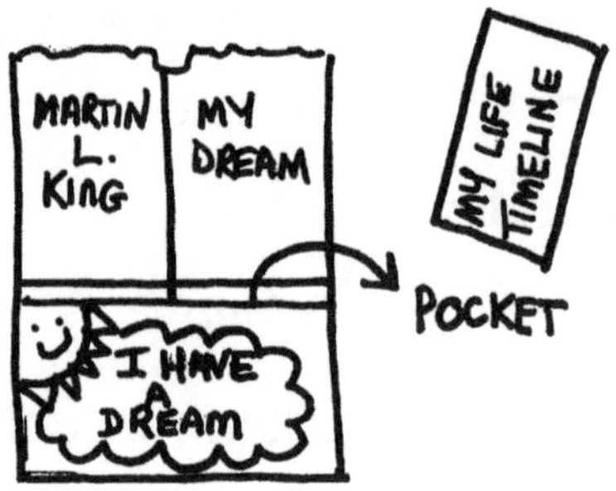

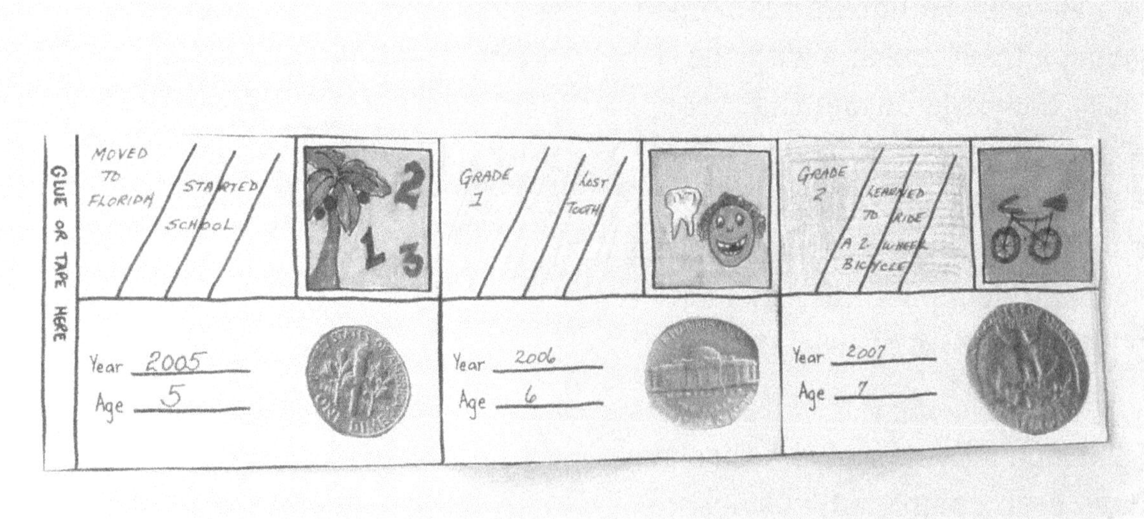

Photograph-Pose Story

Materials needed:

*Digital camera or 36-exposure disposable camera

*8½ in. x 11 in. white paper

*8½ in. x 11 in. lined paper

*Glue

*Crayons, markers, or colored pencils

*Photo album with magnetic pages

Instructions:

(1) Take photos of students doing different actions. Example: Bungee jumping, driving a spaceship, etc.

(2) Teachers should cut around each photo so the only remaining part is the student. The students will use this picture to create a story and illustration of them doing the action shown.

(3) Students will use the 8½ in. x 11 in. white paper to create a background picture. Example: If they are a bungee jumper, they should draw things up in the sky.

Suggestions for kindergarten teachers:

*You may need to suggest some actions if students have difficulty thinking of their own.

*You will also need to cut around the outside of their photos to will prevent them from cutting an arm or leg out of the picture!

Diagrams:

(1)

(2)

(3)

(4) Students will glue the photo to their illustration and create a story to go along with it. These pictures and stories look really great displayed in a magnetic photo album.

(4)

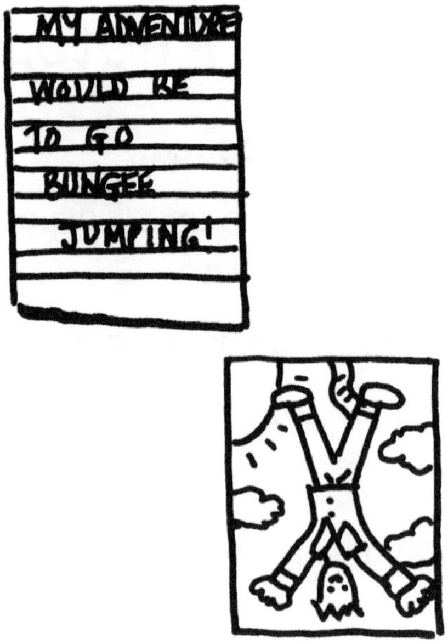

My Special Dream

Materials needed:

*My Special Dream blackline master (p. 172)

*Crayons, markers, or colored pencils

*Glue stick

Optional materials:

*Photograph of student posing as if they are sleeping

*Small piece of fabric

*Literature book about dreams or Dr. Martin Luther King

Instructions:

(1) After the teacher reads a story about dreams or holds a class discussion about what Martin Luther King's dream was for the future, students should brainstorm their dreams for the future.

(2) The teacher and students can list these things on chart paper to give students ideas for illustrations.

(3) Give each student a copy of the blackline master. Fold it in half and cut along the lines so the top layer is a little shorter than the bottom layer.

Suggestions for kindergarten teachers:

*You may want to cut out the blanket area for the students.

*Many of the younger students may not know who Martin Luther King was, so it will be necessary to read or tell about him before doing this activity.

Diagrams:

(1)

(2)

(3)

(4) On the bottom layer, draw a picture or glue on a photo of the student sleeping.

(5) Use the crayons, markers, or colored pencils to decorate the top layer to look like a blanket, and open it to the bottom layer, where students should write or draw about their dream for the future.

(6) Have the students share their dream pictures with the class and compare them to Martin Luther King's dreams.

(4)

(5)

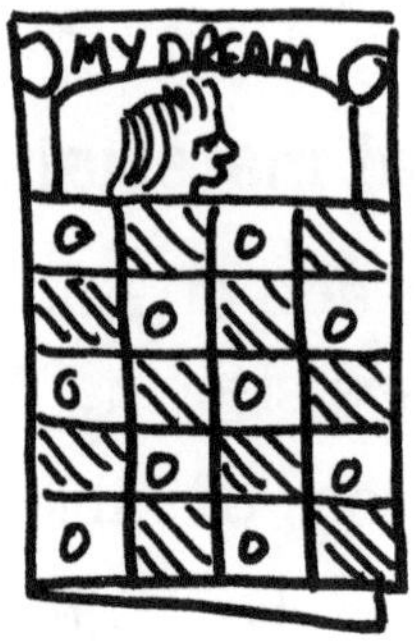

Activity Cards

Coin Timeline

*Look at your Coin Timeline and write a story about the events that have happened in your life.

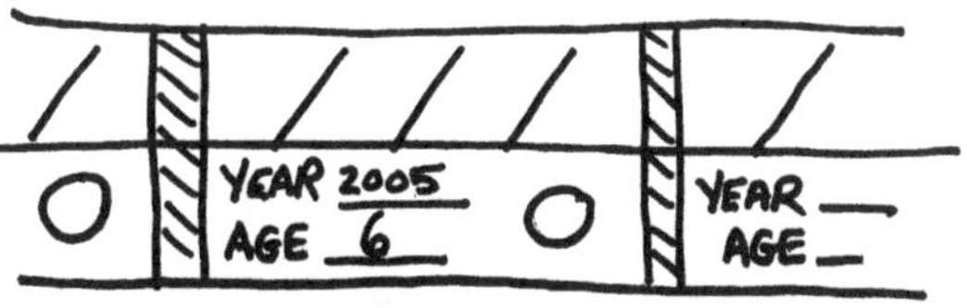

*Compare the story you wrote to the stories of other people in your class.

Coin Timeline

*Now that you have made a timeline of your life, think about Martin Luther King's life and pick three years he was alive.

*Make a Coin Timeline for the years you have selected. See if you can find coins for those years.

Activity Cards

Photograph-Pose Story

*Use your photograph and create a drawing of you doing the job you would most like to have when you grow up.

*Explain why you would like this job.

Photograph-Pose Story

*Use your photograph and a picture of Martin Luther King to create a picture of yourself with him.

*Write about what you would say if you could have met Dr. King.

Activity Cards

My Special Dream

*Create a dream drawing using a picture of Martin Luther King sleeping.

*Write about his dreams for the future.

My Dream

*Martin L. King wanted everyone to be equal and fair to each other. Under the blanket, write about how you make other people feel equal and fair.

February

Toolbox

*Toolbox
*Workman's Fanny Pack
*Career See-through Book
*Career Camera

Toolbox

Materials needed:

*Two pieces of cardstock

*Six brass fasteners

*Brown paper grocery bag

*Clear, wide packaging tape

*3 in. x 3 in. square of craft foam

*Toolbox Tools 1 and 2 blackline masters (pp. 173-174)

*Scissors

*Hole puncher

*Glue stick

*Crayons or markers

Instructions:

(1) Lay the brown paper grocery bag horizontally on the table with the flap side down. Cut the top edges of the bag at an angle to look like a toolbox.

(2) Cut an opening in the top of the bag to look like the lid of a toolbox as shown in the diagram.

(3) Tape the open end of the bag closed, leaving the cuts made in steps one and two open.

Suggestions for kindergarten teachers:

*You may want to pre-cut the edges of the toolbox bag, cut the lid, and tape the edge for students.

*This project works best with younger students when they work in a center or small group with teacher or parent-volunteer supervision.

*It's best NOT to try to complete this project in one class.

Diagrams:

(1)

(2)

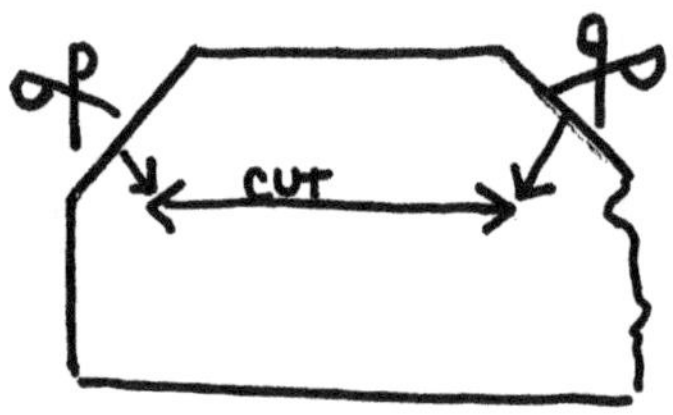

(3)

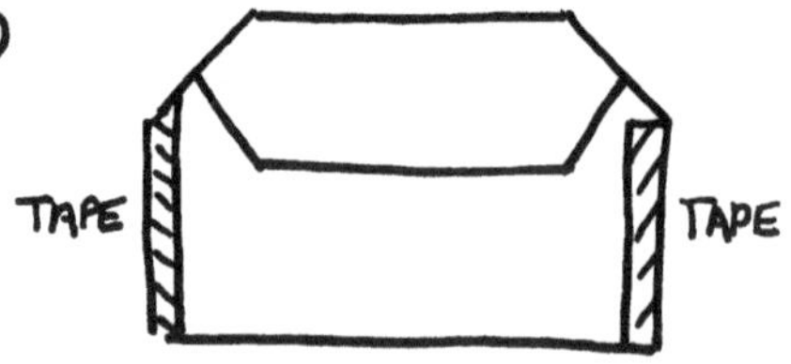

(4) Use one sheet of the cardstock to make a handle for the toolbox. Cut the handle out and attach it to the top edge of the bag with four of the brass fasteners.

(5) Cut the craft foam piece into a latch and attach it to the bag with the remaining brass fasteners.

(6) Fold the other piece of cardstock horizontally and tape down the short edges to create a pocket.

(7) Tape the cardstock pocket to the front of the bag for additional storage.

(8) Color, cut, and glue the tools to the front of the toolbox.

(4)

(5)

(6)

(7)

(8)

How to Use the Toolbox

*Unit of study - Students keep the "tools" of any subject in their Toolboxes. Example: For reading, vocabulary can be kept for each story. For math, basic facts can be stored.

*Storage - Projects, homework, and manipulatives can be stored in the toolbox.

*Paper-tool holder - Use paper tools (hammers, saws, or wrenches) to write vocabulary, rules, and notes from study units.

*Use measuring tape to make a ruler. Attach it to the bag to measure objects in the classroom.

February Writing Suggestions

*Write about someone or something you love.

*What is the best thing about you? Describe your best qualities.

*Explain how to make your favorite sundae. Give step-by-step directions and add illustrations, too.

*What are the "tools" you need to write a good story? Explain what the "tools" are and how to use them.

Workman's Fanny Pack

Materials needed:

*Brown paper lunch bag

*Clear, wide packaging tape

*Survey tape

*Scissors

*Crayons, markers, or colored pencils

Instructions:

(1) Open the bag by putting both hands inside and pressing the pleats outward until flat.

(2) Pull the bottom flap to the back and tape it down with the clear, wide packaging tape.

(3) Fold the top of the bag toward you about halfway down its length. Cut up both sides of the turned-down flap. Cut off the flap that's underneath, allowing only the top flap to remain.

Suggestions for kindergarten teachers:

*Students will need to be assisted with the cutting on this project and placing the survey tape through the slits.

Diagrams:

(1)

(2)

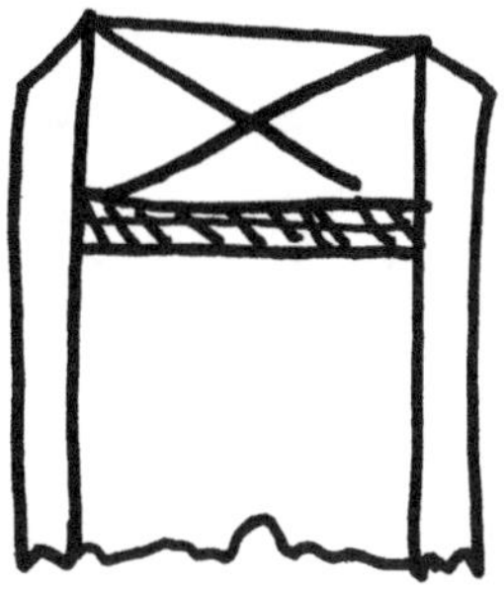

(3)

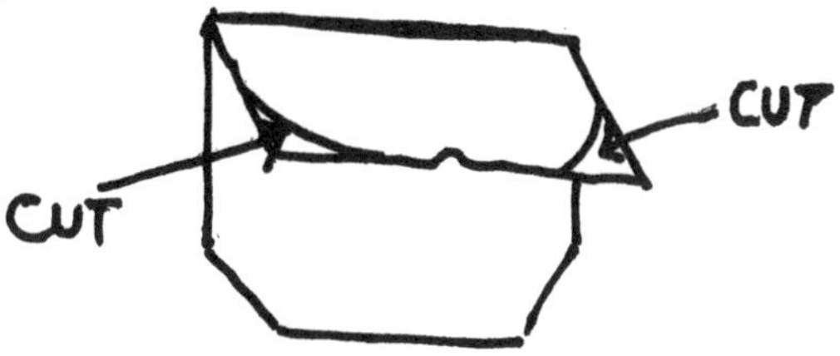

(4) Cut two slits in the back of the bag as illustrated. Insert survey tape into one side and out the other to make a waist strap.

(5) Decorate the fanny pack to match the unit of study. To go with the February theme, you can make a tool belt to go with the toolbox. This tool belt can also be stored in the toolbox.

(4)

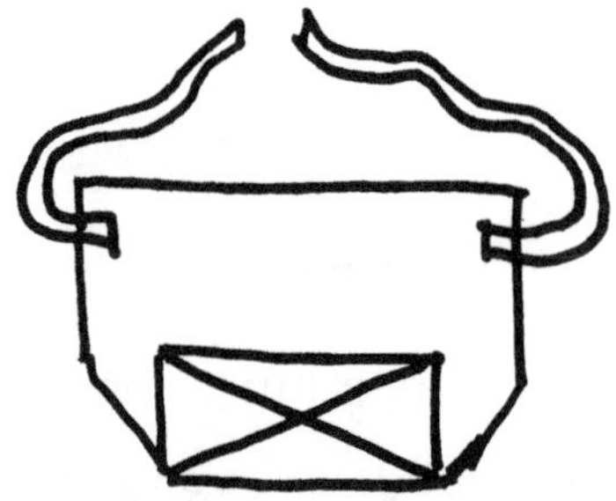

(5)

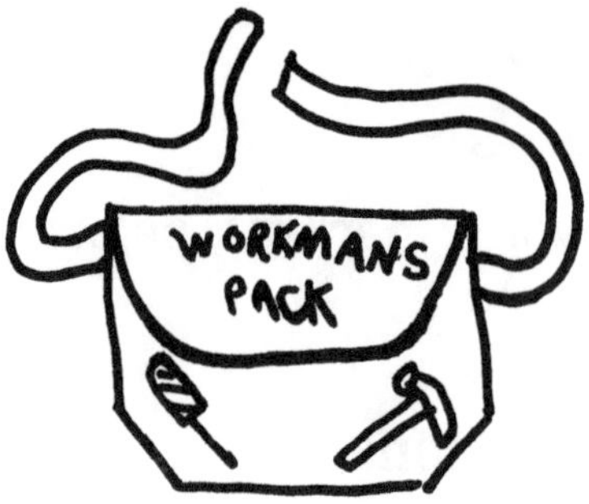

Career See-through Book

Materials needed:

*11 in. x 17 in. paper

*Scissors

*Markers, crayons, or colored pencils

*Laminating machine

Optional materials:

*Face blackline master (p. 175)

Instructions:

(1) Have students brainstorm different careers that they may want to pursue in the future. Make a list of these different careers and talk about the uniform or items they might wear or need.

(2) Place 11 in. x 17 in. paper vertically on the desk. For younger students, the teacher may draw a face circle or use the blackline master.

(3) Students should draw around the face circle (this will be cut away).

(4) Cut the circle out.

Suggestions for kindergarten teachers:

*You may want to trace and cut the face circle in the center of the paper for each student. It is best to color first and then cut it out.

Diagrams:

(1)

(2)

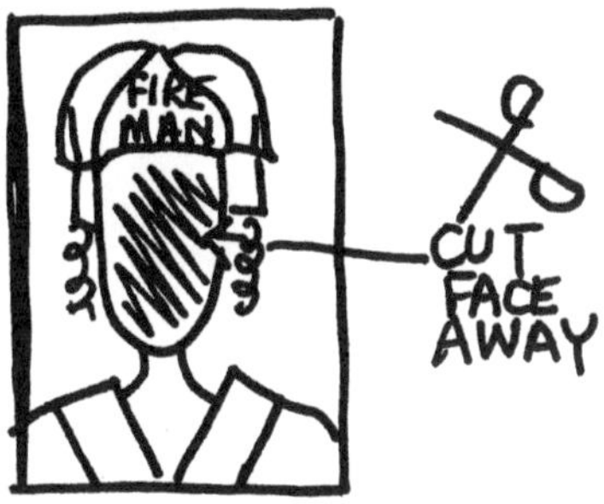

(3)

(5) Laminate the illustrated 11 in. x 17 in. sheet. Students can put their face through it like a mask.

Career suggestions:

*Chef

*Police officer

*Mail carrier

*Hairstylist

*Teacher

*Firefighter

*Scuba diver

Career Camera

Materials needed:

*Career Camera 1 and 2 blackline masters (pp. 176-177)

*One yard of survey tape

*One pipe cleaner

*Hole puncher

*Crayons, markers, or colored pencils

Instructions:

(1) Cut out the camera blackline master, which may be run off on colored or white copy paper. Carefully cut around the flashbulb and stand the bulb up. Fold it in half along the center line.

(2) Cut out the snapshots blackline masters and slip them into the camera.

(3) Hole punch through the camera and the snapshots.

(4) Cut the pipe cleaner in half and insert one half into each hole at the top of the camera. Twist each pipe cleaner to form a loop.

Suggestions for kindergarten teachers:

*You may want to cut out the camera and cut around the flash for the students.

*Some younger students may need to be assisted putting the camera together.

Diagrams:

(1)

(2)

(3)

(4)

(5) Insert the survey tape through the loops and tie it to make a neck strap.

(6) On the snapshot blacklines, students should illustrate things that go along with the career they have chosen. Below each picture, they should write about the snapshot. If more room for writing is needed, continue on the back side of the snapshot.

(7) The outside of the camera may be colored or decorated, and a title may be added to go with the selected career.

(5)

(6)

(7)

Activity Cards

Workman's Fanny Pack

*Inside your Workman's Fanny Pack, draw pictures of things you would need to do a job that you might have in the future.

*Allow a friend to look at what you have drawn and guess your job.

Workman's Fanny Pack

*Cut out pictures from magazines or newspapers of people doing different jobs.

*Pick your favorite and tell why you would like this job.

Activity Cards

Career See-through Book

*Make a Career See-through Book for a character from your favorite story.

*Would you like to be that character? Why or why not?

Write about it.

Career See-through Book

*When you grow up, you might have two jobs, like a mother and a mail carrier or a father and teacher.

*Create two Career See-through faces and tell about how you would do both jobs.

Activity Cards

Career Camera

*Inside your camera, draw pictures of some jobs you think are very interesting.

*On the lines under the snapshots, write about each job.

Career Camera

*Pick one job that you would like to have one day. Draw pictures of things you would do for that job.

*Write some of the facts you know about that job.

March

Up-in-the-Air Bag

*Up-in-the-Air Bag
*Cloud Tissue-Box Windows
*Kite and Other Shape Books
*Up-in-the-Air/Right-on-the-Ground
Plane Ticket

Up-in-the-Air Bag

Materials needed:

*Large brown paper grocery bag

*One cheap paper plate

* Up-in-the-Air Bag Hot-Air Balloon blackline master (p. 178)

*One brass fastener

*Crayons or markers

*Scissors

*Glue stick

*Stapler

Instructions:

Hot-air balloon side:

(1) Flip the large brown grocery bag to the side with the flap. Staple the sides of the flap so that it will create a pocket.

(2) On the flap, draw the basket of a hot-air balloon.

Above the basket, draw the balloon and strings that attach the balloon and basket to each other.

(3) Use the labels from the blackline master and glue them on the appropriate parts of the hot-air balloon.

Suggestions for kindergarten teachers:

*You will need to guide students to create the drawings on the bag.

*For the windmill, draw the triangles that students will cut out for themselves.

*Assist students in attaching the brass fastener for the windmill.

Diagrams:

(1)

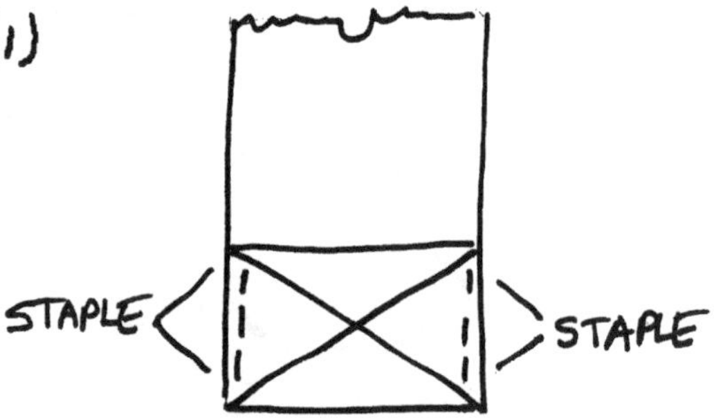

(2)

(3)

Windmill side:

(1) Flip the bag to the other side (the side without the flap). Draw the building that supports the windmill. It may be helpful to provide students with pictures or examples of this.

(2) Cut four triangles from the edges of the paper plate to near the center. The plate will now look like the paddles of a windmill.

(3) Attach the windmill to the bag with the brass fastener. Place the paper plate on top of the bag and then push the brass fastener through the plate and top layer of the bag.

(1)

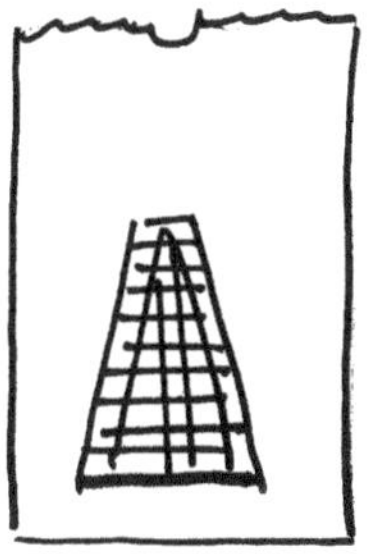

(2)

(3)

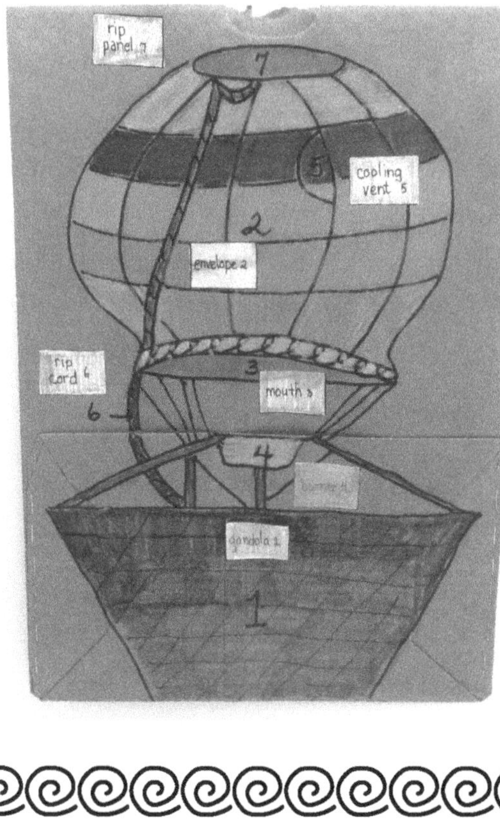

How to Use the Up-in-the-Air Bag

*Up-in-the-air log - Read about things or people that are mostly "up in the air." Keep a log of the books read in your bag.

*Keep a cloud journal - Make the clouds out of cotton, glue them to different pieces of paper, and tell what kind of weather is coming.

*Make paper kites - Write a story on the kite about what makes you as happy as a kite soaring in the wind. Attach ribbons to a string at the bottom of the kite. Keep your kite in the bag.

*Flight timeline - Make a timeline of your "flight" in the classroom. Make it on adding-machine tape and attach it to your bag.

March Writing Suggestions

*Design a new postage stamp. What would be on it? Why? Write about it.

*Look out your window and write about what you see.

*Pick a partner. Write a story together about something strange that came from space into your backyard.

*Weave a flying carpet with construction paper strips. Add fringe on the two ends. Be creative. Take students' pictures seated or lying down as if on a flying carpet, or make a large flying carpet and put all students' pictures on it. Students can write about their "flight" on the carpet.

Cloud Tissue-Box Windows

Materials needed:

*Square facial tissue boxes – one for each type of cloud selected

*Cloud Tissue-Box Windows 1 and 2 blackline masters (pp. 179-180)

*Scissors

*Glue Stick

*Cellophane tape

*One page protector

*Crayons, markers, or colored pencils

Instructions:

(1) Carefully pull apart the glued seams of each box so that it lies flat. For each box, fold the top onto one of the sides so that the pattern is around the oval and on the side facing out.

(2) Cut around the square top and side of the box to form a small picture frame. Remove the slit pieces of plastic from center. Use the page protector to make a new plastic window and tape it into place.

(3) Color and cut out selected clouds from the blackline master.

Suggestions for kindergarten teachers:

*You may want to cut and create the windows for students and then have them put the clouds inside.

*The windows can also be created in small groups with supervised instruction.

Diagrams:

(1)

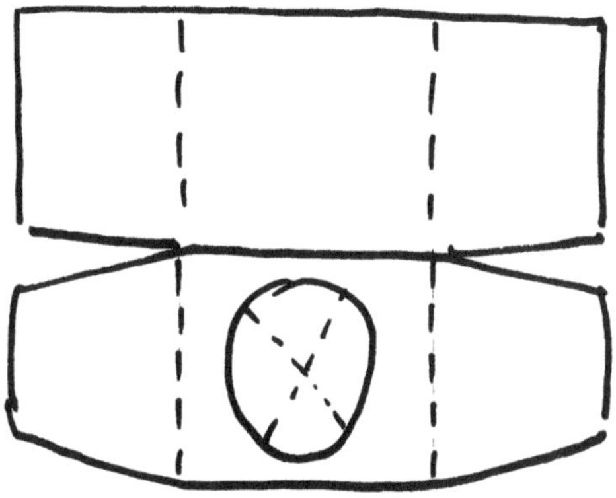

(2)

(3)

(4) Use the glue stick to glue the clouds into place on the inside of the window. Do not glue the top layer down; that way, the windows can be opened and closed to show the names of the clouds.

(4)

(5) Once your cloud windows have been created, glue each one onto the Up-in-the-Air Bag. The clouds can be glued on one or both sides of the bag.

(5)

***Optional:** The clouds can be made from cotton or other soft material to add texture to them.

Kite and Other Shape Books

Materials needed:

*Two sheets of cardstock, 8½ in. x 11 in. or larger

*Writing paper for inside book

*Two pipe cleaners cut in half

*Scissors

*Hole-puncher

*Crayons, markers, or colored pencils

Instructions:

(1) Brainstorm with students things that are seen up in the air. Examples: sun, stars, moon, clouds, rainbow, airplanes, birds, flying machines, helicopter, hot-air balloons, kites, rockets, etc. Select your favorite for which to create a book. These can be individual books or a class book.

(2) Cut both pieces of cardstock and the writing paper into the desired shape.

(3) Draw details on and color both pieces of cardstock. Add a title and author name to the front cover.

Suggestions for kindergarten teachers:

*You may want to pre-cut the cover and writing/drawing pages for students. This book may be best made as a class book and not individual books.

*Allow each student to take a turn sharing the book at home.

Diagrams:

(1)

(2)

(3)

(4) Hole punch through both the back and front cover pieces and all writing pages to be placed inside the book. Depending on the shape of the book, you may want one to four holes.

(4)

(5) Place the pages inside the book in the correct order. Match up the hole punches and slide a pipe cleaner piece in each hole. Twist each pipe cleaner into a loop and secure.

(5)

***Optional binding rings:** You can also use chicken rings (found in a feed store), shower curtain rings, electrical ties, or key rings to bind this book.

Up-in-the-Air/Right-on-the-Ground Plane Ticket

Materials needed:

*9 in. x 12 in. sheet of construction paper (any color)

*Up-in-the-Air/Right-on-the-Ground Airline Ticket 1 and 2 blackline masters (pp. 181-182)

*Scissors

*Glue stick or stapler

*Pencils

*Crayons, markers, or colored pencils

Instructions:

(1) Place the 9 in. x 12 in. construction paper vertically on the table.

(2) Fold the construction paper in half vertically.

(3) Fold the top corner of the top layer on the diagonal and cut it away.

(4) Staple or glue the edges of the top layer to the bottom layer to create a pocket.

(5) Cut out the blackline master of the plane ticket and fill in details about the imaginary flight.

Suggestions for kindergarten teachers:

*You will probably want some parent volunteers to assist you with the set-up of the classroom.

*Show students who have never been on an airplane pictures of the inside and outside of a plane.

Diagrams:

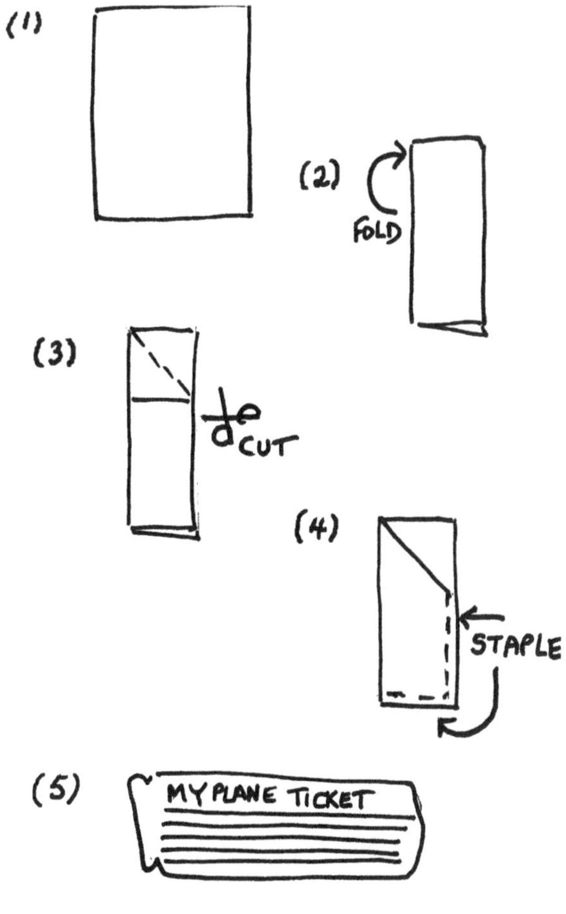

Imaginary Flight Agenda:

(1) Move all the desks, tables, and chairs to the side of the classroom to create a large, open space. Outline the shape of an airplane's interior on the floor with masking tape. Arrange chairs in rows to simulate airplane seats.

(2) Prior to takeoff, sell tickets for this flight. Encourage students to bring luggage and dress up as a passenger: ties and briefcases for traveling businessmen, purses and briefcases for ladies, strollers and baby dolls for mommies.

(3) Assume the role of captain and lead children through an imaginary flight. Have them fasten seatbelts and prepare for takeoff. Select one or two students to be flight attendants who serve snacks as they walk down the aisle. If you have a parent who works for an airline, they could assist in class or provide airplane items.

(4) Once airborne, have students pretend to look out the window and describe what they see. Can they see anything on the ground?

(5) After you have landed and deplaned, invite students to illustrate their version of an aerial view.

Activity Cards

Cloud Tissue-Box Windows

*Think about things you see up in the air. Use the tissue-box tops to make some windows.

*Glue paper to the inside and draw things that can be seen up in the air.

*Attach them to your Up-in-the-Air Bag.

Cloud Tissue-Box Windows

*Think about things that you can see from your bedroom window.

*Attach paper inside the tissue-box windows and draw pictures of your favorite things you like to look at from your bedroom window.

Activity Cards

Kite and Other Shape Books

*Kites can be in many shapes and sizes.

*Create a kite in an unusual shape. Do you think your kite design will fly? Why or why not?

Kite and Other Shape Books

*In Japan, children make kites for Children's Day. The oldest child in the family gets the biggest kite. Think about your family.

*Make a kite for each child in your family. The oldest gets the biggest kite and the youngest gets the smallest.

Activity Cards

Up-in-the-Air/Right-on-the-Ground Plane Ticket

*Now that you have gone on an imaginary flight, create a travel poster about your visit.

*Your poster can include: the name of the place, a map of the place, things you did there, etc.

Up-in-the-Air/Right-on-the-Ground Plane Ticket

*Make a handle out of a small piece of paper and glue it on the open side of a file folder.

*Pretend this is your suitcase. Draw some things you would take on a trip and write about them.

April

Shower-Flower Backpack

*Shower-Flower Backpack
*Water-Cycle Bracelet
*Seed-Packet Book
*Cassette-Box Planter

Shower-Flower Backpack

Materials needed:

*Two brown paper grocery bags

*One ½-inch square of sticky-back Velcro®

*Clear, wide packaging tape

*Glue

*Scissors

*Crayons, markers, or colored pencils

*5 feet of survey tape

*Shower Flower Backpack 1-4 blackline masters (pp. 183-186)

Instructions:

(1) Cut 4 inches off the top of each bag. Using the clear, wide packaging tape, tape the bottom flap of each bag up to form pockets.

(2) Tape the bottom of the top bag to the top of the top of the bottom bag.

(3) Decorate the top pocket to illustrate the water cycle and the bottom to show a garden and parts of a flower. Label the "Shower" and "Flower."

Suggestions for kindergarten teachers:

*You may want to use a paper cutter to cut the 4 inches off the top of each bag for students.

*The taping can be done by the teacher or in small groups.

*Younger students will need help with the survey-tape straps.

Diagrams:

(1)

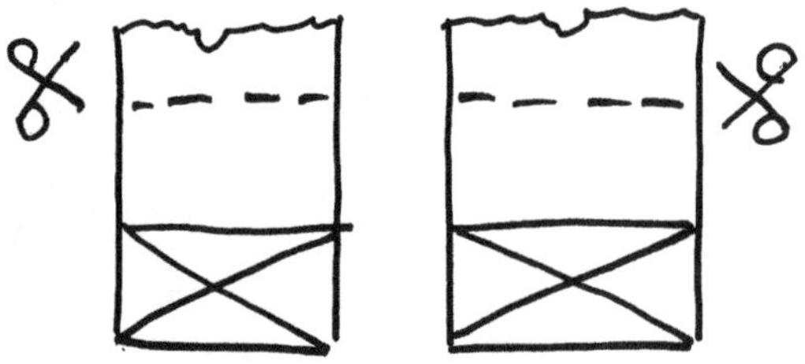

(2)

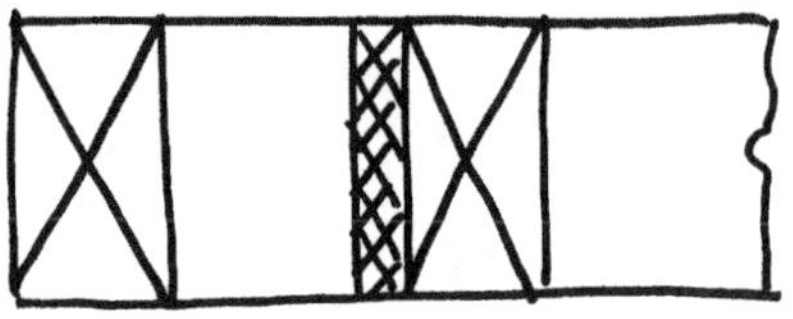

(3)

(4) Fold the bags forward and then apply sticky-back Velcro® to keep them closed together. Cut slits as shown. Thread the survey tape through the slits to create the backpack straps.

(5) Decorate the front of the backpack using the crayons, markers, or colored pencils.

(6) Throughout the month, store successive projects in the backpack pockets.

(4)

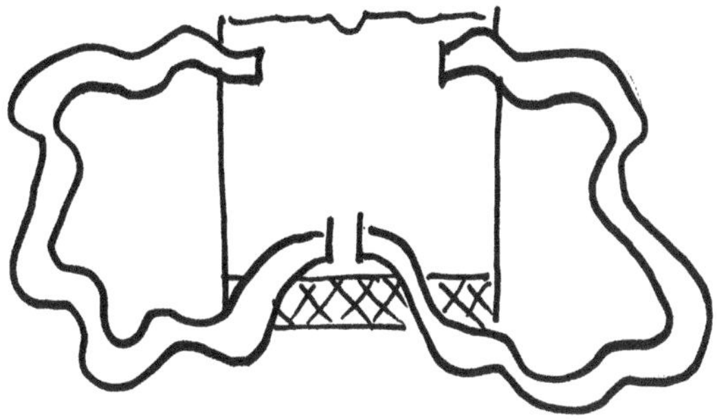

(5)

How to Use the Shower-Flower Backpack

*Unit of study - Students keep the unit of study in the bag. For science, keep plant drawings inside and attach the Water-Cycle Bracelet to the bag.

*Felt board - Make a felt board that can be added to the bag. Students can use felt pieces to show the water cycle and interfacing to make the clouds.

*Fruits and vegetables - Keep a list of fruits and vegetable. Create a table showing how these plants grow-above the ground or below, on vines or as bulbs, and their colors.

*Page-protector plants - Staple four half-sheets of page protectors together with a construction-paper back. Starting from the back, show the parts of a plant, fruit, or vegetable. These will build on top of each other.

April Writing Suggestions

*Tell all about what you do or could do on a rainy day.

*Make a song up about the weather or water cycle. Use your vocabulary words.

*You have discovered a new flowering plant. Where was it found? Describe it. What can it be used for?

*Create a story where it is raining something other than water. Be creative!

Water-Cycle Bracelet

Materials needed:

*One black pipe cleaner

*Assorted colors of pony beads

Instructions:

(1) Twist one end of the pipe cleaner around your finger to form a loop.

(2) String each bead on to form an order or sequence from nature. Some examples:

The water cycle:

yellow = sun

white = clouds

clear = evaporation

blue = water (lakes, oceans)

green = land

Parts of a plant:

white = roots

light green = sprout

medium green = stalk

dark green = leaves

pink = blossom

red = flower

Suggestions for kindergarten teachers:

*Make the loop in each pipe cleaner for younger students and talk about why each color is used.

Diagrams:

(1)

(2)

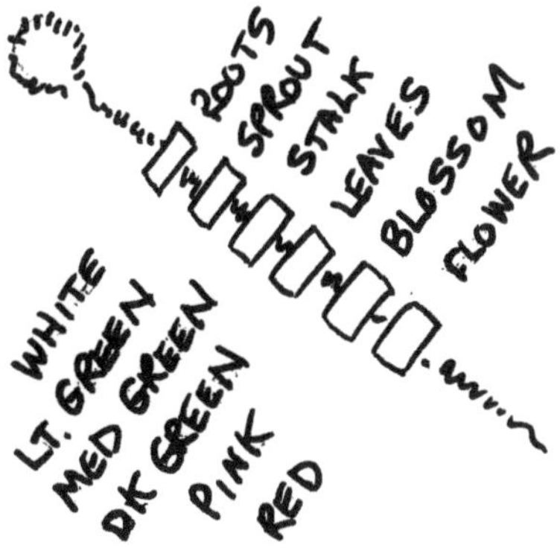

Environments:

white = arctic regions

brown = desert regions

blue = oceans

green = rainforests

tan = mountain regions

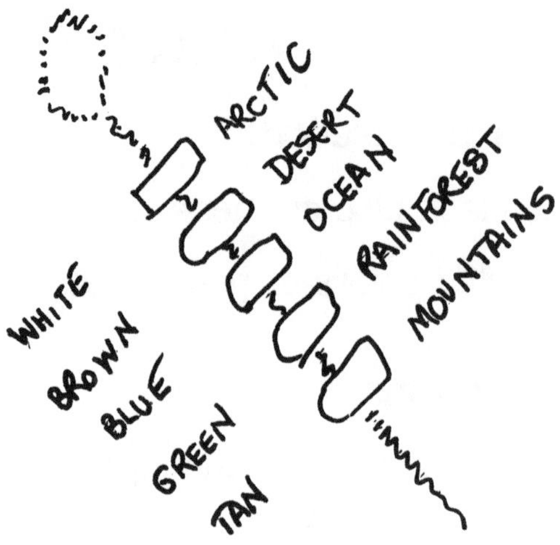

***Attribute bracelet** – Use a different color bead to represent student attributes: blue for a boy, pink for a girl, brown if they have a dog, black if they have a cat, red if reading is their favorite subject, purple if math is their favorite subject, etc.

Seed-Packet Book

Materials needed:

*11 in. x 17 in. paper

*Construction paper in assorted colors

*Seed-Packet Book 1 and 2 blackline masters (pp. 187-188)

*Scissors

*Glue

*Crayons, markers, or colored pencils

*Stapler or tape

Instructions:

(1) Fold the 11 in. x 17 in. paper vertically. (We call this fold a hamburger fold.)

(2) Staple or tape the edge to create a pocket.

(3) Illustrate the front of the pocket with a type of plant, real or imaginary.

(4) On back of the pocket, write all the important facts and information about the plant. Does it like sun or shade? Does it like to be dry or wet? How big will your plant grow?

Suggestions for kindergarten teachers:

*You may want to fold and staple or tape packets for the students.

*This project may be best done using the same type of seeds with all students.

Diagrams:

(1)

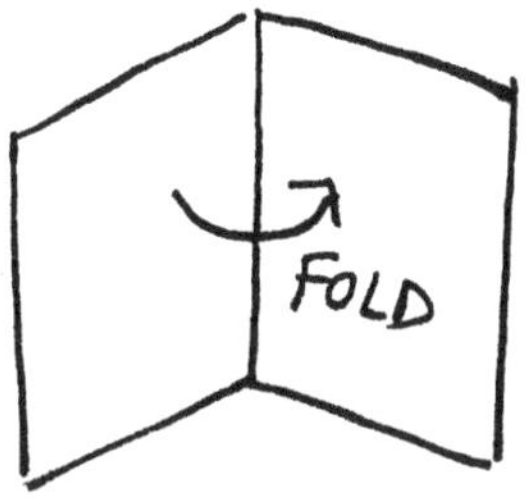

(2)

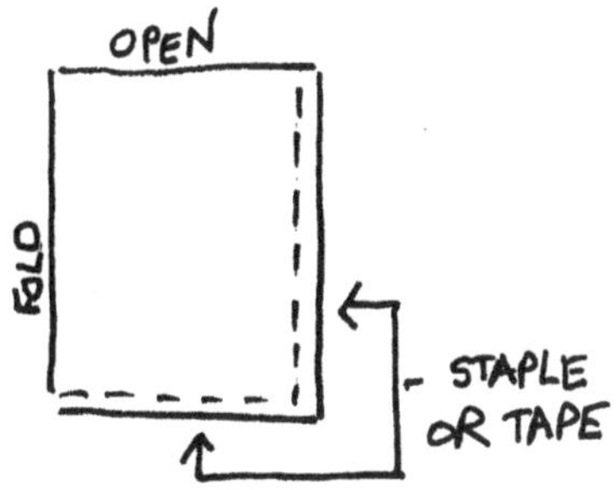

(3)

(4)

(5) On the inside of the pocket, make a plant from the construction paper. You can label all the parts and pull it out so it appears to be growing.

***Helpful hints** – Bring some different seed packets in to class. Have students look at them and discuss the kinds of information found on the outside of the package. This would also be an excellent activity to do along with planting the seeds and watching them grow. The students can also make a plant log book inside the packet to record daily observations about their plant inside.

(5)

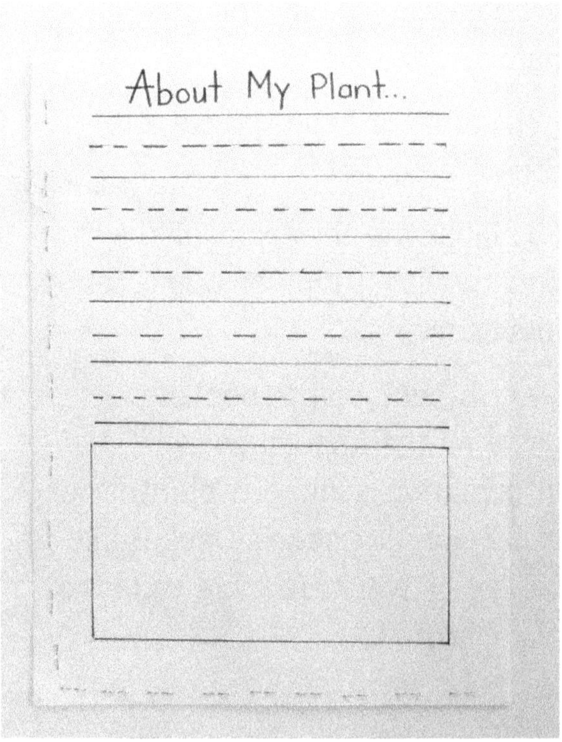

Cassette-Box Planter

Materials needed:

*Empty cassette-tape box

*Small piece of compressed sponge or kitchen sponge

*Pencil

*Hole-puncher

*Fine-tip black marker

*Sticky-back blank label

*Easy-to-germinate seeds

Instructions:

(1) To speed germination of the seeds, soak them in a cup of water for about three hours.

(2) Cut the sponge into a 2½ in. x 4 in. rectangle. Open the cassette box. Rub the pencil over the post points on the inside. Place the sponge in the cassette box and gently close the box. The pencil lead will mark the placement of the posts.

(3) Remove the sponge from the case and hole punch the pencil marks.

(4) Dampen the sponge and then place both the sponge and the seeds into the cassette box.

Suggestions for kindergarten teachers:

*You will need to pre-cut the sponges and punch the holes to fit the containers for students.

*With younger students, it is best to use larger seeds like bean or sunflower seeds.

Diagrams:

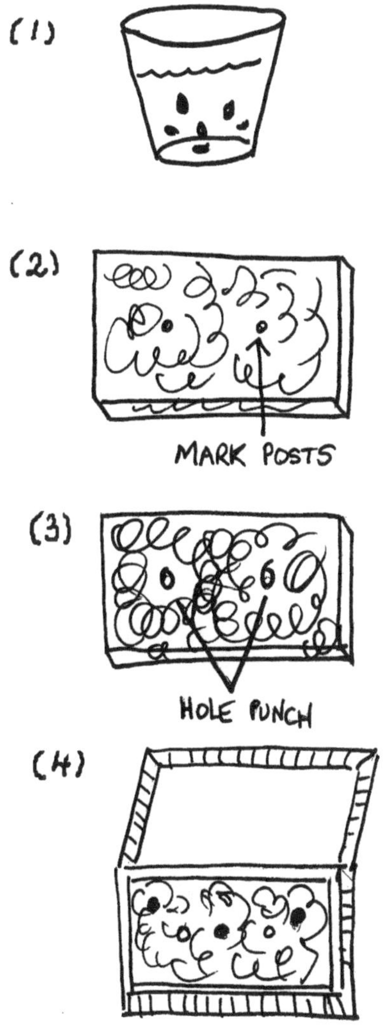

(5) Use the fine-tip black marker and sticky-back label to label the seed starter with your name, date, and the kind of seed you planted.

(6) Watch your seeds grow! When seeds are large enough, transplant them into the ground or flower pot.

***Helpful hints** – The Bag Ladies also like to use cassette boxes as storage boxes for small game pieces, manipulatives, and other small items. If you cannot find enough cassette boxes, any small, clear, plastic box will work for this project. We have also used small, clear, plastic bottles and added a string so students can wear their seeds as they grow.

(5)

(6)

Activity Cards

Water-Cycle Bracelet

*Using your Water-Cycle Bracelet to remind you of the steps of the water cycle, create an illustration to show the water-cycle process.

*Use your drawing to explain the water cycle to a friend.

Water-Cycle Bracelet

*Now that you have made a Water-Cycle Bracelet, try to use other colors of beads and create a bracelet that shows all the parts of a flower. Pick a color for each part: roots, leaves, sprout, blossom, stalk, flower.

Activity Cards

Seed-Packet Book

*Now that you have created a seed packet, draw a picture of what a garden might look like with your plant growing in it.

*You can also include other plants in your garden.

Seed-Packet Book

*Write step-by-step directions to explain how to plant a garden.

*Draw a picture to go with each step in your directions.

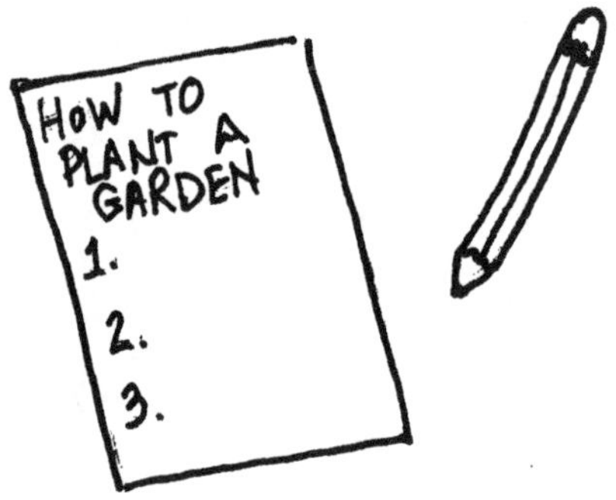

*See if someone can follow your directions.

Activity Cards

Cassette-Box Planter

*Create a daily log on the growth of your seeds. Draw a picture and write about each day's growth in your log.

*How do they look after day 1? Day 2? Day 3? Week 1?

Cassette-Box Planter

*After the seeds begin to take root, carefully remove them from the cassette box.

*Place some dirt in a small container, add the seedlings, and cover with more dirt. Add water and watch your seeds grow!

May

Environment Bag

*Environment Bag
*CD Accordion Book
*Dial-a-Story
*Book-on-a-String

Environment Bag

Materials needed:

*Brown paper grocery bag

*One cheap paper plate

*9 in. x 12 in. construction paper (yellow, green, blue, brown, and white)

*Environment Bag 1-5 blackline masters (pp. 189-193)

*Crayons or markers

*Glue

*Stapler

*Scissors

Instructions:

(1) Cut the construction paper to the following lengths (all pieces should be 9 in. wide):

Yellow – 2 in., green – 4 in., blue – 6 in., brown – 8 in., white – 10 in. Lay the colors in order, with the longest on the bottom and the shortest on top, and staple them to the bottom flap of the bag, creating a step book.

(2) Color the paper plate to resemble the Earth using green and blue crayons. Glue the plate to the bottom flap of the bag. Glue a label on the world that reads "What does my Earth have?"

Suggestions for kindergarten teachers:

*You may want to cut and attach the layers to the bag for students and allow them to insert the proper pictures and labels.

*You can have students complete one layer every few days and learn about that environment as they create the bag.

Diagrams:

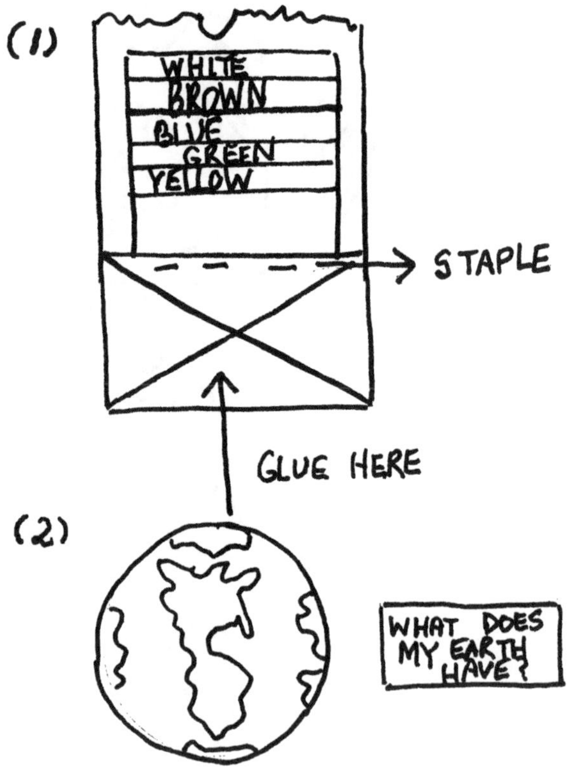

(3) Use the appropriate labels, plant pictures, and animal pictures for each layer of the bag: yellow – desert, green – forest, blue – water, brown – mountains, white – Arctic and Antarctic regions. The edges of the layers can be cut to add details.

(3)

(4) On the brown bag, glue a yellow circle to represent the sun. Allow it to peek out from behind the mountain tops. Characters can be added to the project if desired.

(4)

***Helpful hints** – The back side of the bag can be used for other related projects including the ones for this month. You can extend the environment lesson to include energy, animal food chains and webs, or students' choice. Be creative and let students help choose how to use the back of the bag.

How to Use the Environment Bag

*Unit of study - Use the bag as an organizational tool for the study of environments.

*Make a game - Make index cards of environments, animals, and plants. Sort them by cold areas, hot areas, animals that live under the ground, animals that live above the ground, and plants that live in that environment. Make up a game to be played with two players. Keep your game in the bag.

*Choose one environment - Create a mural of your chosen environment on a piece of 11 in. x 17 in. paper.

*Desk brainstorm - Brainstorm as many animals as you can and put them into the correct environments written on cards on your desk.

May Writing Suggestions

*List ways you can help the environment. Describe how the class can help.

*Write a graduation speech about leaving the grade you are in and moving on to the next grade. What will you miss? What are you looking forward to?

*Design the perfect playground. Explain what is on it and why.

*Think about different environments, then draw a setting. Now write all about your setting.

CD Accordion Book

Materials needed:

*Empty CD cases

*CD Accordion Book 1 and 2 blackline masters (pp. 194-195)

*Glue or cellophane tape

*Crayons, markers, or colored pencils

*4½ in. x 4½ in. piece of cardstock

*Scissors

Instructions:

(1) Cut out the desired number of CDs from the blackline master in pairs that overlap. Remember to cut the center hole out from each CD so they will fit into the case. Glue or tape the tabs together to form a "string" of CDs.

(2) Add illustrations, words, sentences, and/or stories to each CD and color them. Make sure the CDs follow a sequential order from left to right. Students might choose one environment to draw and write about or they could include information from all of the environments.

Suggestions for kindergarten teachers:

*You may want to cut out the blackline masters for younger students, including the center circles on the CDs.

Diagrams:

(1)

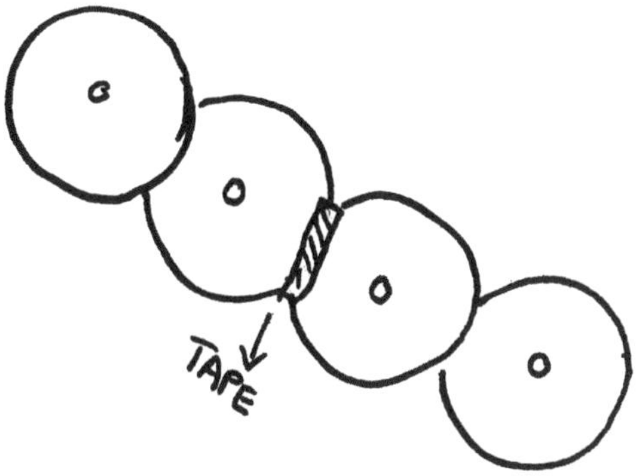

(2)

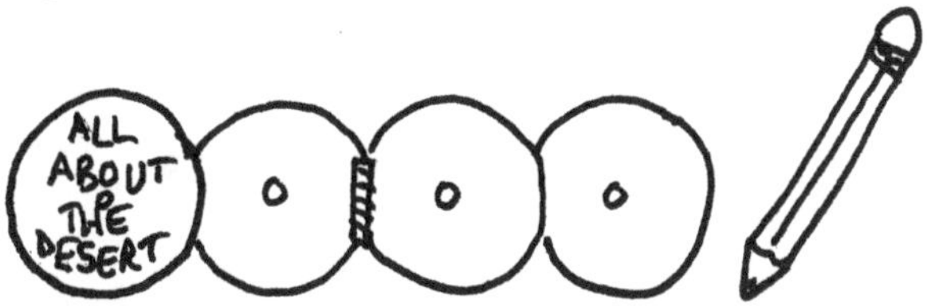

(3) Start with the first picture and fold the CDs to form an accordion-style booklet.

(4) Place the booklet inside the CD case so that, by pulling on the top CD, the booklet will unfold in sequential order.

(5) Design and illustrate a cover or title page on the cardstock square that shows the topic of study for the CD "story."

(3)

(4)

(5)

Dial-a-Story

Materials needed:

*Two cheap paper plates

*One brass fastener

*Scissors

*Crayons, markers, or colored pencils

Instructions:

(1) Trim the ruffled edge off of one of the paper plates.

(2) Locate the center of each plate and mark it with a dot.

(3) Fold the plate without the ruffle in half. Cut a triangle-shaped window from this plate. (Do not cut too close to the center dot or edge of the plate.)

(4) Open the cut paper plate and place it on top of the uncut plate. Fasten them together with a brass fastener.

(5) To decorate, students can create an illustration on the small plate and write a sequence of events in the window. Turn the plate to see each event.

Suggestions for kindergarten teachers:

*You will need to assist younger students with cutting and inserting the brass fastener.

Diagrams:

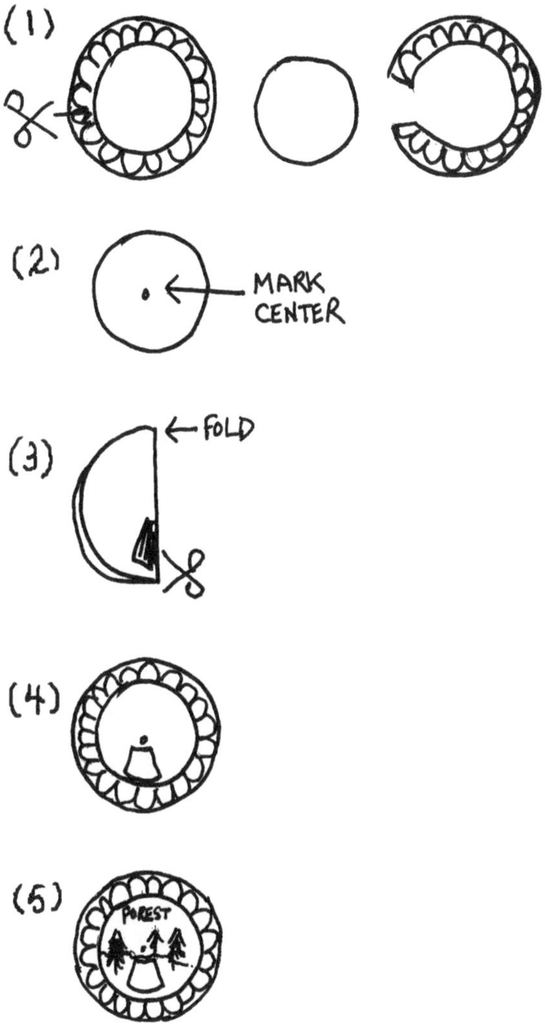

***Helpful hint** – This activity would be a great opportunity for students to chose their favorite environment and research plants and animals that live in that environment. Another idea would be to read a story that goes with a selected environment and design the Dial-a-Story to go along with it. The Dial-a-Story can then be attached to the back of the Environment Bag.

Book-on-a-String

Materials needed:

*1 yard of leather or plastic cord

*Scissors

*Hole-puncher

*Three or more 3 in. x 5 in. blank index cards

*One elastic pony tail band

*6 pony beads in assorted colors

Instructions:

(1) Stack the index cards on top of each other. Hold them horizontally in front of you.

(2) Fold the stacked index cards in half as shown in the diagram.

(3) Cut a ¾-inch slit at the top and bottom of the fold through all the cards.

(4) Unfold the cards and roll them horizontally, but do not crease them.

(5) Slide the pony tail band over the rolled cards, stopping at the slits.

Suggestions for kindergarten teachers:

*You may need to assist students with punching the holes in the cards. They will also need assistance with tying the knot at the end of the cord.

Diagrams:

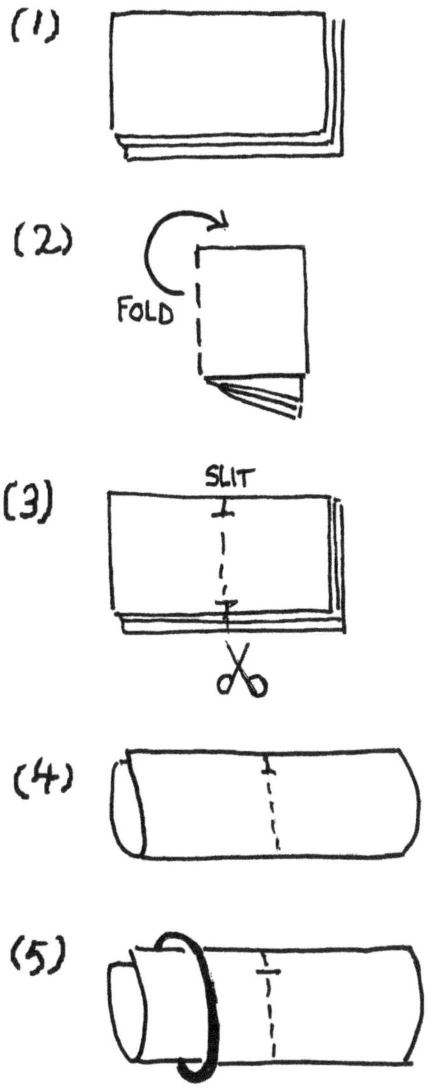

(6) Open the cards up and allow the band to stay in the slits. Refold the cards on the fold line.

(7) Punch a hole through the cards in the top left corner near the slit.

(8) Slide the cord through the hole and add beads to decorate it. Finally, tie the cord with a slip knot.

(9) Inside the book, write important facts, information, or vocabulary words from the environments you studied.

(6)

(7)

(8)

Activity Cards

CD Accordion Book

*Pick an environment you would like to learn more about.

*Use the CD Accordion Book to record all the information you learned about that environment.

*Share what you have learned.

CD Accordion Book

*Create pictures on each CD page so that they tell a story. Make sure there is a sequence to the story.

*Add at least one sentence to each page that will tell the story.

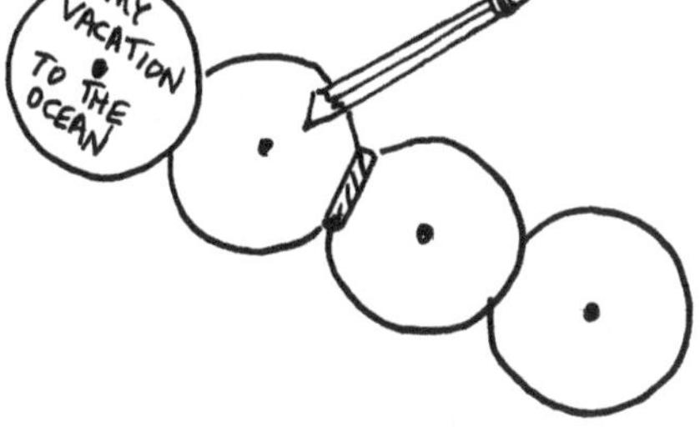

Activity Cards

Dial-a-Story

*On the top paper plate, draw the plants in one of the environments you learned about this month.

*On the bottom paper plate, draw different animals found in that environment. Then turn the dial and draw more pictures.

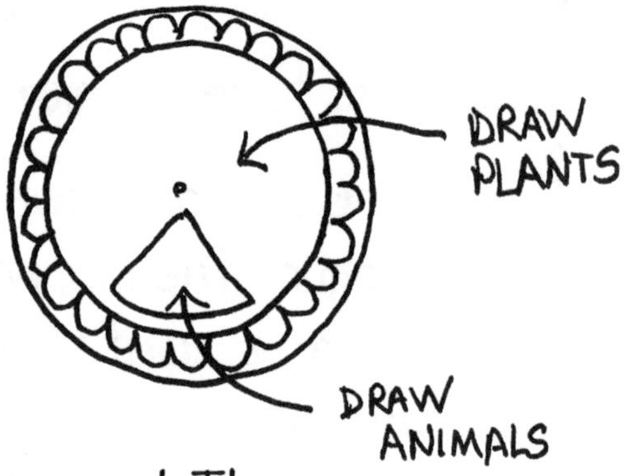

Dial-a-Story

*Use a green and blue crayon and make the top plate look like the Earth.

*In the window, make small pictures of the environments you learned about during this unit.

Activity Cards

Book-on-a-String

*Pick an environment.

*In your Book-on-a-String, write vocabulary words for that environment.

*Add pictures to go with the vocabulary words.

Book-on-a-String

*Think of the interesting facts you have learned about plants and animals.

*Draw pictures and write a sentence about some of your favorite facts.

*Share these with a friend.

Summer

Palm Tree Pocket Bag

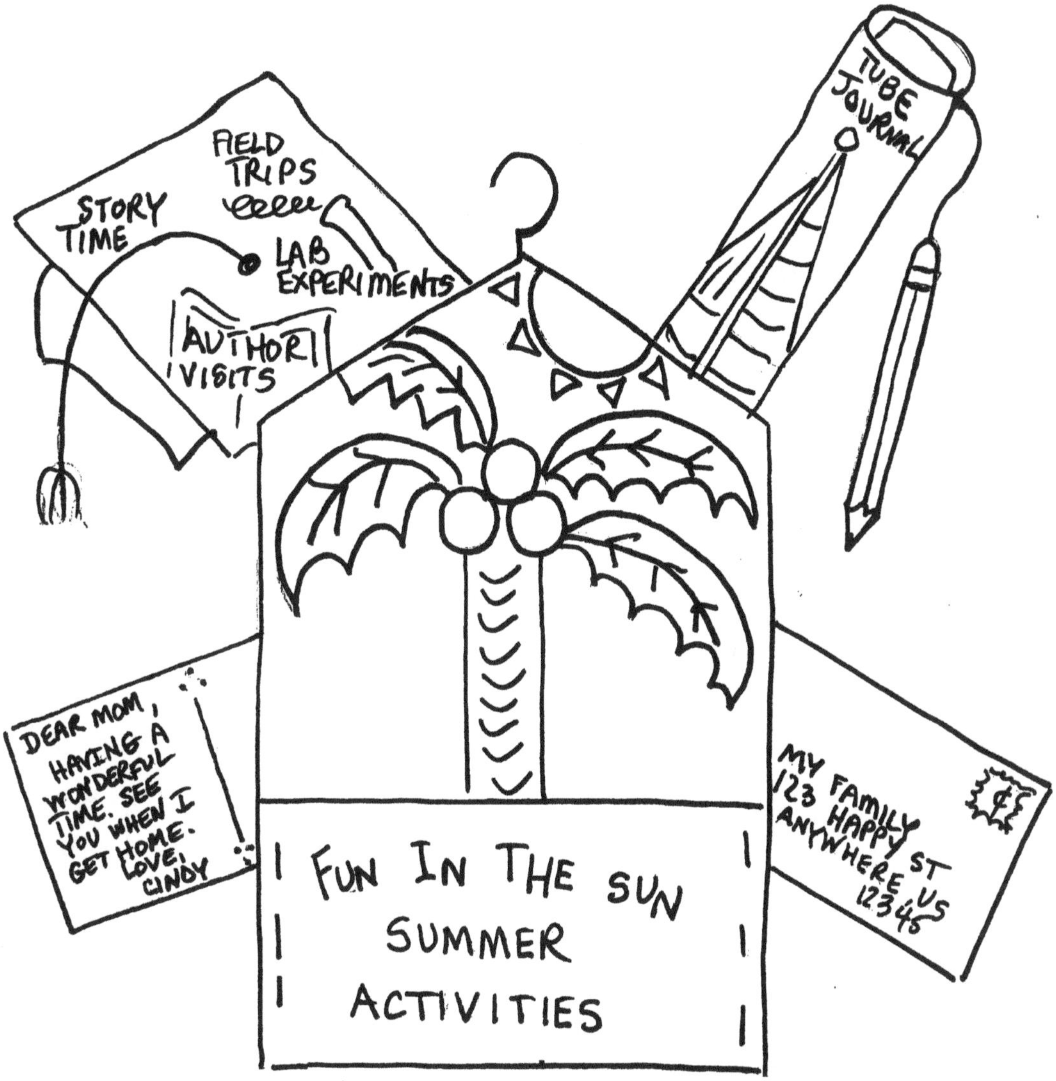

*Palm Tree Pocket Bag
*Journal in a Tube
*Graduation Hat
*Postcard Book
*Magazine-Page Envelope

Palm Tree Pocket Bag

Materials needed:

*One wire clothes hanger

*Brown paper grocery bag

*Stapler

*Green, brown, and blue construction paper

*Palm Tree blackline master (p. 196)

*Glue

*Markers, crayons, or colored pencils

Instructions:

(1) Open up the brown paper bag, and cut up one side and around the bottom of the bag.

(2) Open up the larger piece of the brown paper to lay flat. Throw away the piece that was the bottom.

(3) Lay brown construction paper vertically on the table.

(4) Place the wire clothes hanger at the top of the paper.

(5) Fold the top corners of the brown paper over top of the hanger, and staple into place.

Suggestions for kindergarten teachers:

*You will need to assist the younger students with folding down the top of the bag and stapling the edge. Additional help may be needed to staple the edges of the pocket.

Diagrams:

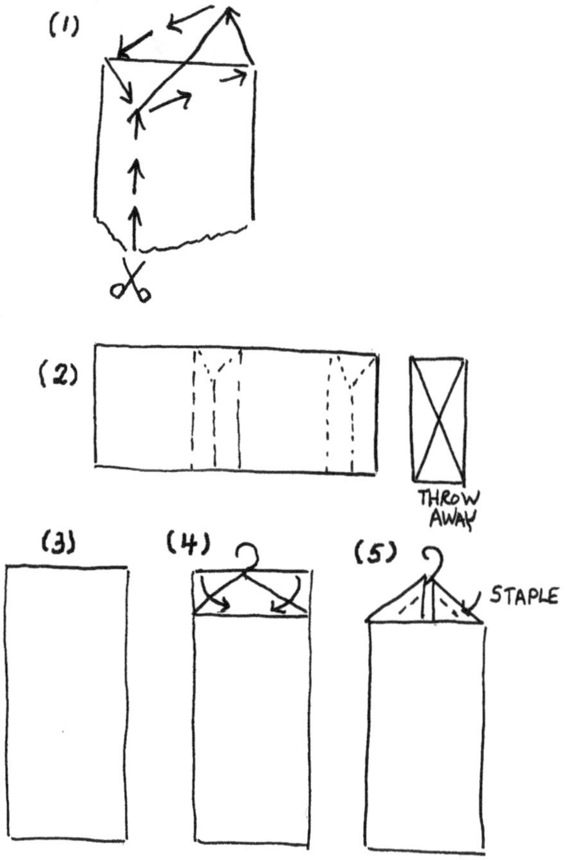

(6) Fold the bottom of the brown paper up twice, approximately six inches each time.

(7) Staple the edges to form a pocket along the bottom of the bag.

(8) Decorate the front of the bag with a palm tree and label it “Fun in the Sun” Summer Activities.

(9) Use the pocket to place some activities in for students to do over summer vacation. These could include summer reading lists, practice math problems, or other summer projects.

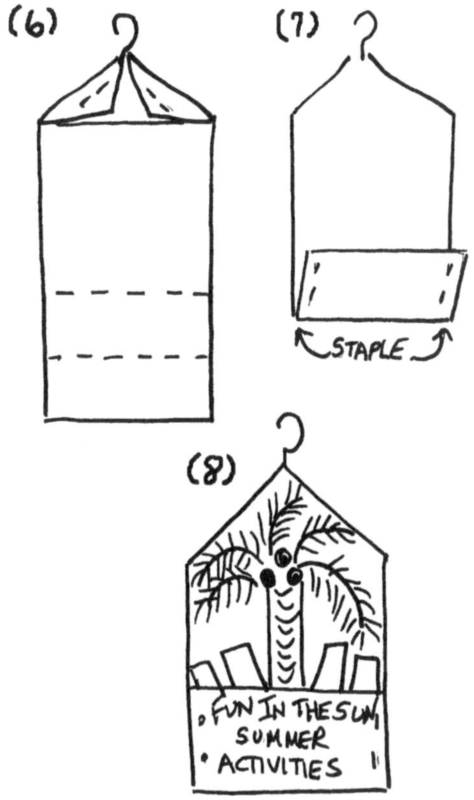

How to Use the Palm Tree Pocket Bag

*A survival kit - This kit, which can be taken home in the Palm Tree Pocket Bag, can include book suggestions, math facts, and writing ideas to practice over the summer.

*Collect postcards - These can be of places you go, or you can ask your friends and relatives to send a postcard from wherever they travel over the summer.

*Make a game - Practice skills for the next grade level. Keep the pieces for the game in the pockets.

*Keep a book list - Write down all the books you want to read over the summer on small pieces of paper. Keep the slips of paper in the pockets. When you finish one book, pull out the next slip to reveal the next book you will read.

Summer Writing Suggestions

*Describe your summer activities. Write them in a scrapbook/diary style. Explain the activity, who you went with, and what you did. Add your own special feelings about your day.

*Create the perfect vacation. Where would it be? What would you do?

*Make a list of words that tell about summer. Write a describing word (or two) to tell about all the words in your list. Write a paragraph using as many of the new words as you can.

*Think of a person you would like to meet. Explain why you want to meet this person. What would you ask him/her? What would you tell him/her?

Journal in a Tube

Materials needed:

*Long, cardboard paper-towel or gift-wrap tube

*Heavy brown paper

*Crayons, markers, or colored pencils

*Glue

*Scissors

*Paper stapled together as a journal

*Scraps of twine, beads, feathers, craft foam, and/or gift wrap

Instructions:

(1) Decorate the heavy brown paper, and glue or tape it to the outside of the tube. Tie scraps of twine to either end, and add beads and feathers to the ends of the tube.

(2) On the front of the paper stapled together as a journal, design a cover to go along with a topic, or use the journal as an end-of-the-year autograph book.

(3) Hole punch the edge of the journal, and attach twine or string long enough to stick out of the end of the tube. Feathers or beads can also be added to decorate the string.

Suggestions for kindergarten teachers:

*You may not want to add the twine with beads and feathers if it will be difficult for the students to tie these things on. In place of these, think of other items students can decorate with, like large wooden beads and plastic lacing.

*You can tie a pencil on each journal for the students.

Diagrams:

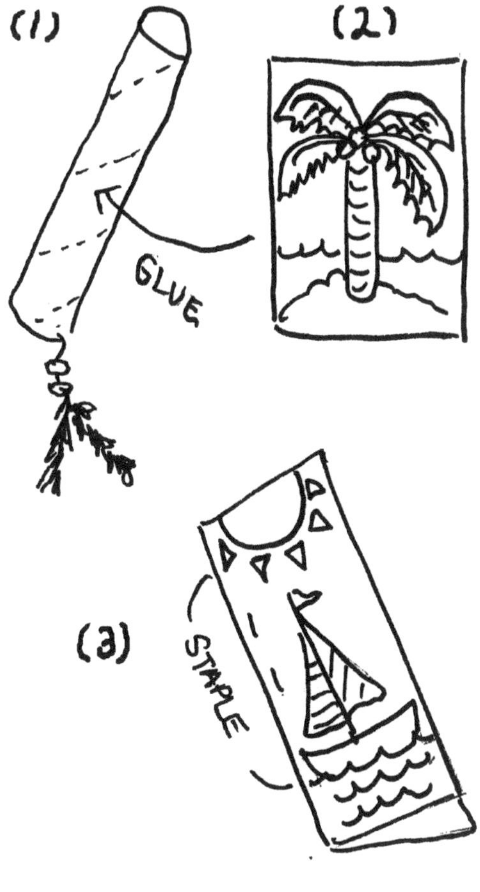

(4) Carefully roll up the journal tight enough to fit inside of the tube. Be sure to allow the string to hang out the end of the tube so the journal can be pulled out easily.

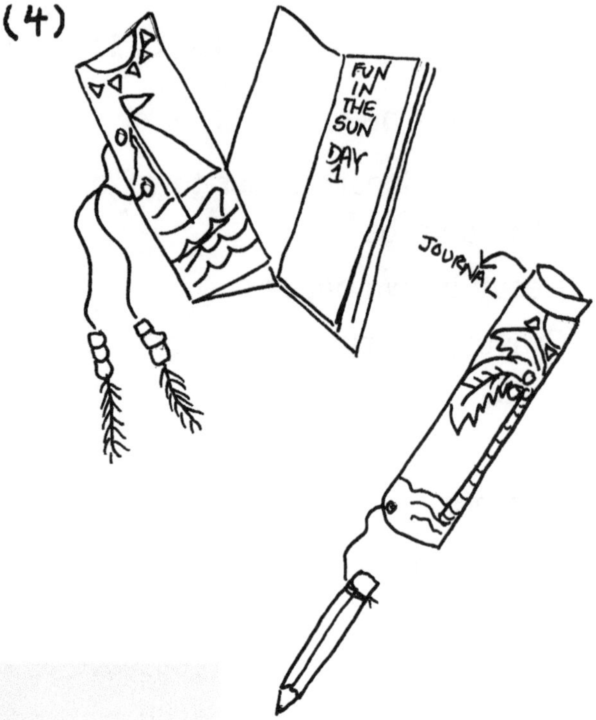

***Optional:** Add a small pencil or pen to the string, so the journal is ready to travel with students. Small golf pencils can be purchased at local office supply stores.

Graduation Hat

Materials needed:

*9 in. x 9 in. piece of tag board in any color

*One paper sentence strip

*2 feet of yarn

*One brass fastener

*Scissors

*Crayons, markers, or colored pencils

*Cellophane tape

Instructions:

(1) Draw pictures or write about your favorite things that happened this school year on the 9 in. x 9 in. square of tag board. You can also allow other students to sign their names on the squares.

(2) Measure around your head with the sentence strip to form a headband. Tape or staple it closed to fit your head.

(3) Place the 9 in. x 9 in. tag board picture-side down on the table. Place the headband on top of the square.

Suggestions for kindergarten teachers:

*You will need to assist the students with attaching the headband to the tag board square.

*You can have students draw on the tag board, and then you can put the hats together for them as a last-day surprise.

Diagrams:

(1)

(2)

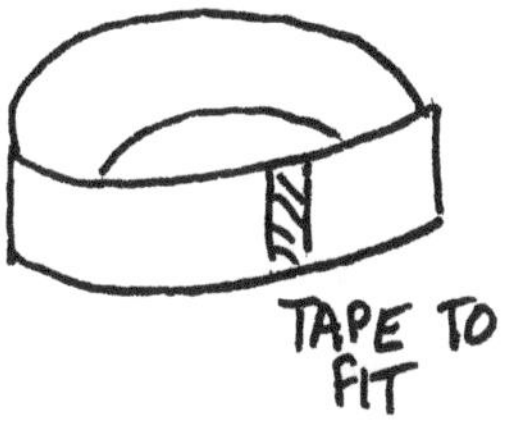

(3)

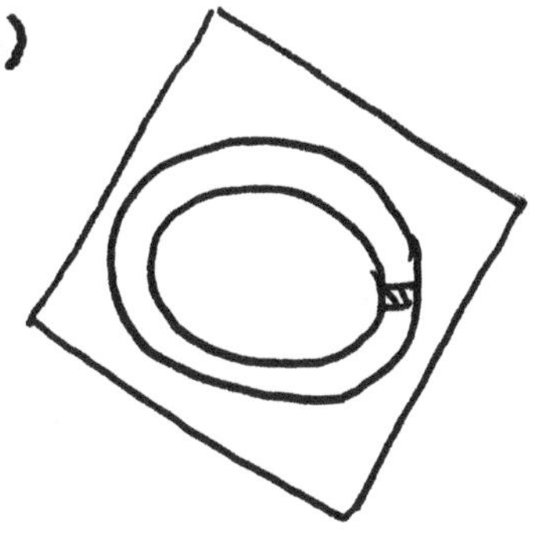

(4) Center the headband on the tag board and tape it in place around the edges.

(5) Using the brass fastener, punch a hole in the center of the tag board square. Push the brass fastener to the other side and open the wings

(6) Cut small pieces of yarn to create a tassel and tie it around the brass fastener.

(7) Students can now wear their graduation hats home on the last day of school.

(4)

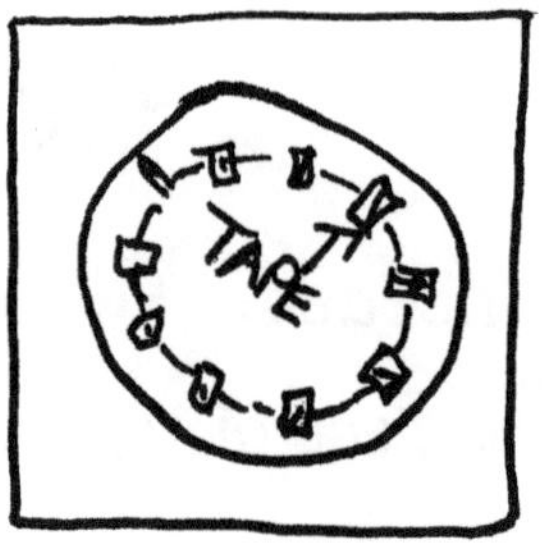

(5)

(6)

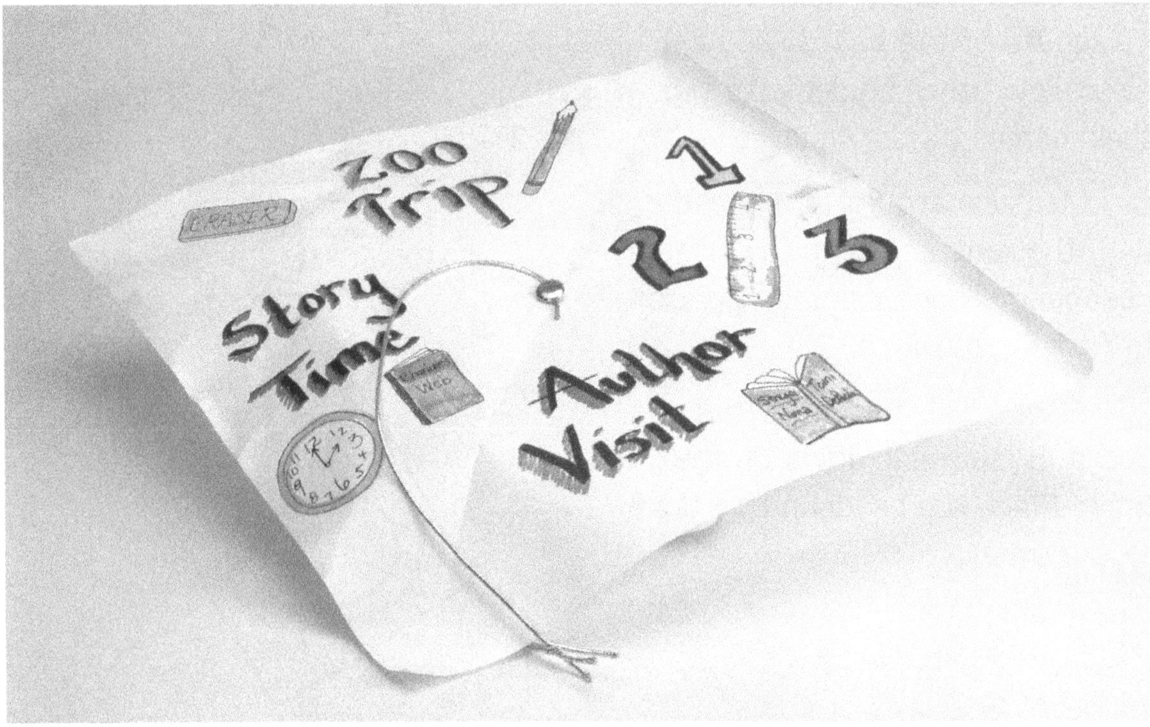

Postcard Book

Materials needed:

*Postcard Book blackline master (p. 197)

*Crayons, markers, or colored pencils

Instructions:

(1) First, model the correct format of writing on a postcard (return address, recipient's address, message).

(2) Have students decide on a theme for their postcards and illustrate the front. (We like to have students watercolor-paint the background after creating a crayon picture using the crayon-resist technique.)

(3) On the back of the postcard, students create a short letter and learn to write an address properly.

(4) Students can mail their postcards, turn them into a class book, or put them in their Palm Tree Pocket Bags to send to someone over the summer.

Suggestions for kindergarten teachers:

*Enlarge the blackline master onto legal or 11 in. x 17 in. copy paper for younger students to use.

Diagrams:

(1)

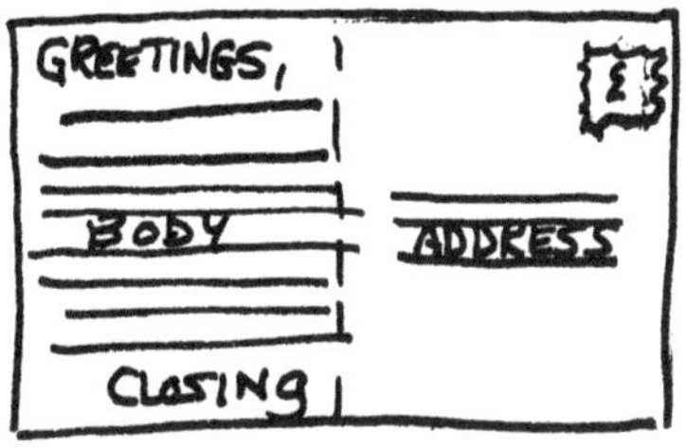

(2)

(3)

(4)

MY
POSTCARD
COLLECTION

Magazine-Page Envelope

Materials needed:

*Colorful picture from a magazine with few words on it

*Scissors

*Glue stick

*Blank address label stickers

*Pencils or pens

*One sheet of 8½ in. x 11 in. lined paper

Instructions:

(1) Place the magazine page picture-side down and vertically on the table. Fold into thirds, with the bottom two thirds larger than the top third.

(2) Open the magazine page up and fold the vertical edges in one inch on each side. Cut away the top and bottom two vertical rectangles as shown in the diagram.

(3) Fold the middle two rectangles toward the center and glue them down. Fold the bottom section up and glue it down. The top two edges can be angle-cut like an envelope flap.

Suggestions for kindergarten teachers:

*You may want to create these envelopes in small groups when students first learn how to make them. After students have done this a few times, they should be able to do it in larger groups or independently.

Diagrams:

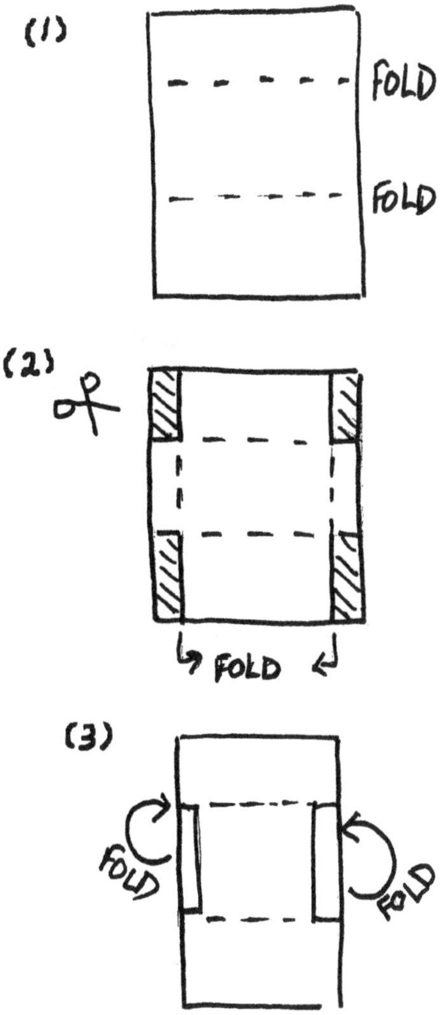

(4) Place the address label on the front. Write a letter and place it inside the envelope.

(4)

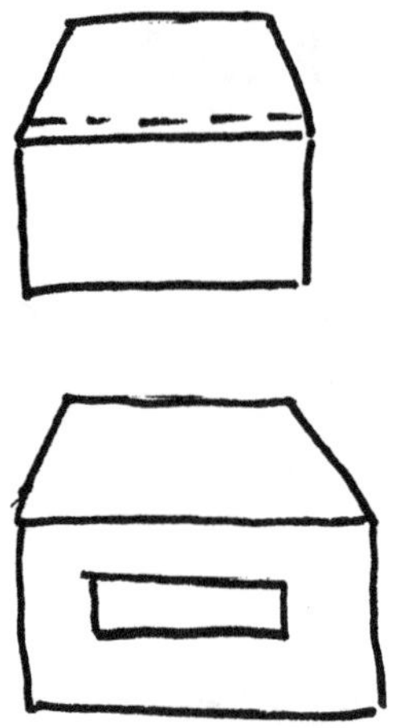

Activity Cards

Journal in a Tube

*Make a goal that you will write twice a week over the summer.

*Write four June dates, four July dates, and four August dates. Try to remember to write in the journal each week this summer.

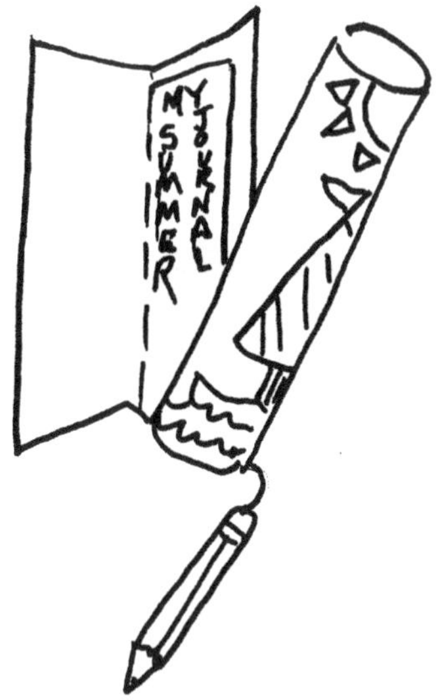

Journal in a Tube

*An autograph book is a book where you have people write nice things about you and sign their name.

*Ask people at your school to write in and autograph your tube journal. Read it when you feel lonely.

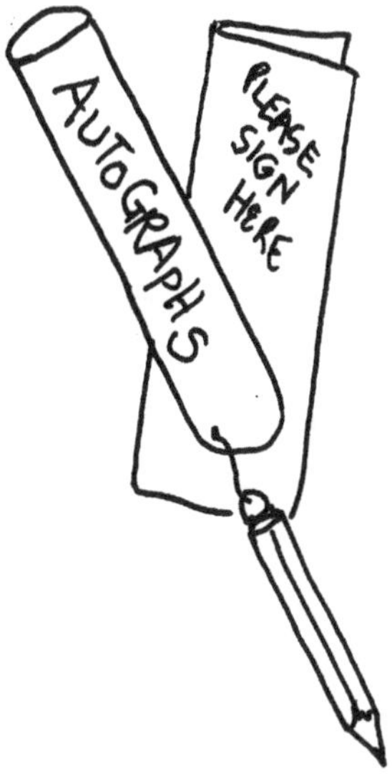

Activity Cards

Graduation Hat

*Next year will bring all new experiences. Think about your favorite parts of this year.

*Write or draw a picture that includes your hopes and wishes for next school year.

Graduation Hat

*Think of some of your favorite experiences this year.

*Draw pictures or write about what you really liked most about this year on your hat.

*Share your hat with your family.

Activity Cards

Postcard Book

*Postcards are a quick, easy way to stay in touch over the summer.

*Decorate a set of postcards and address them to people you might not see over the summer. Write on them while away from school, and mail or share them later.

Magazine-Page Envelope

*Make a whole set of Magazine-Page Envelopes.

*Decorate paper to match each envelope.

*Place them in your Palm Tree Pocket Bag and write summer letters.

Blackline Masters

October
Explorer Book Cover

October
Discovery Boat Pattern

October
Autumn Tree

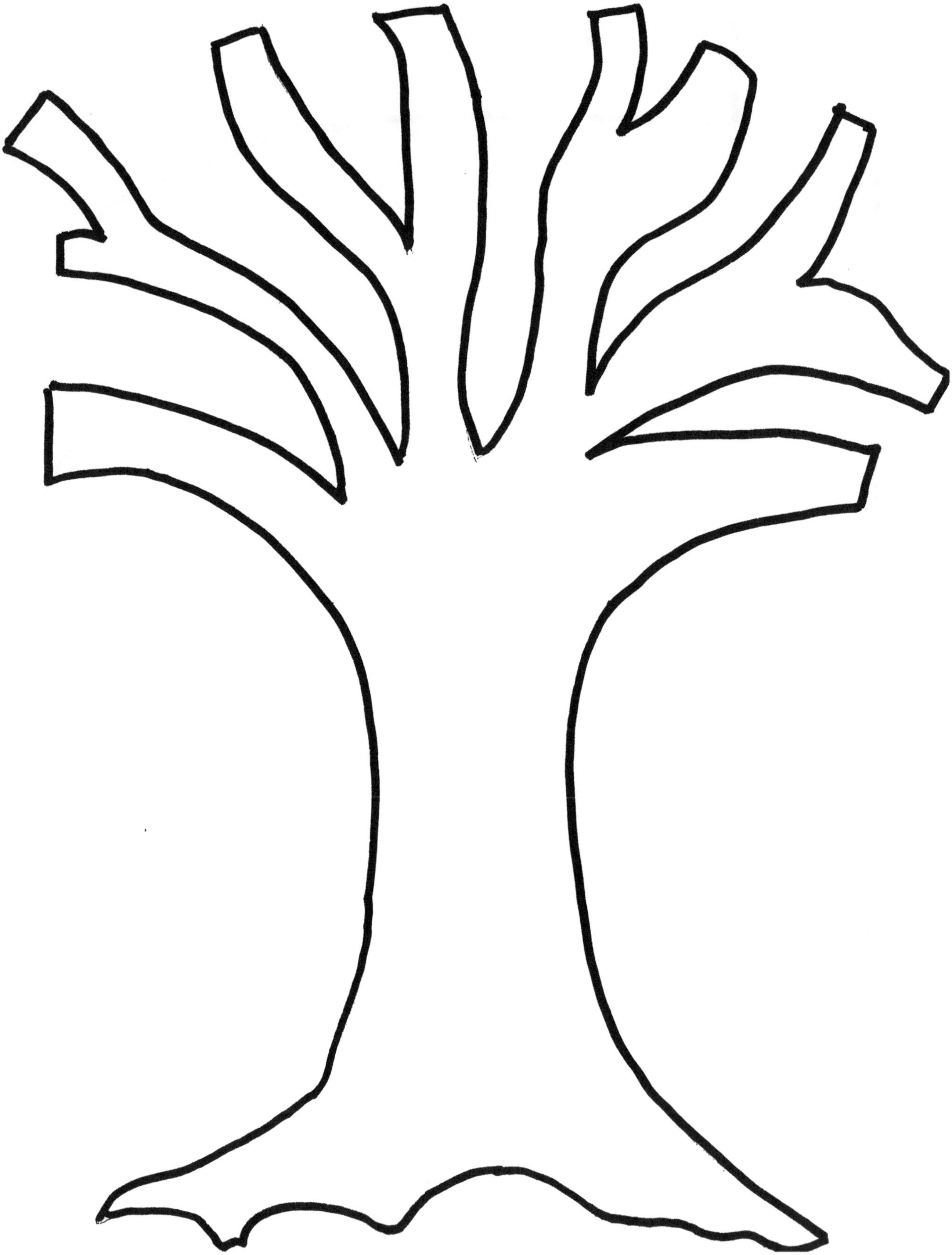

October
Discovery Day Hat Ship Pattern

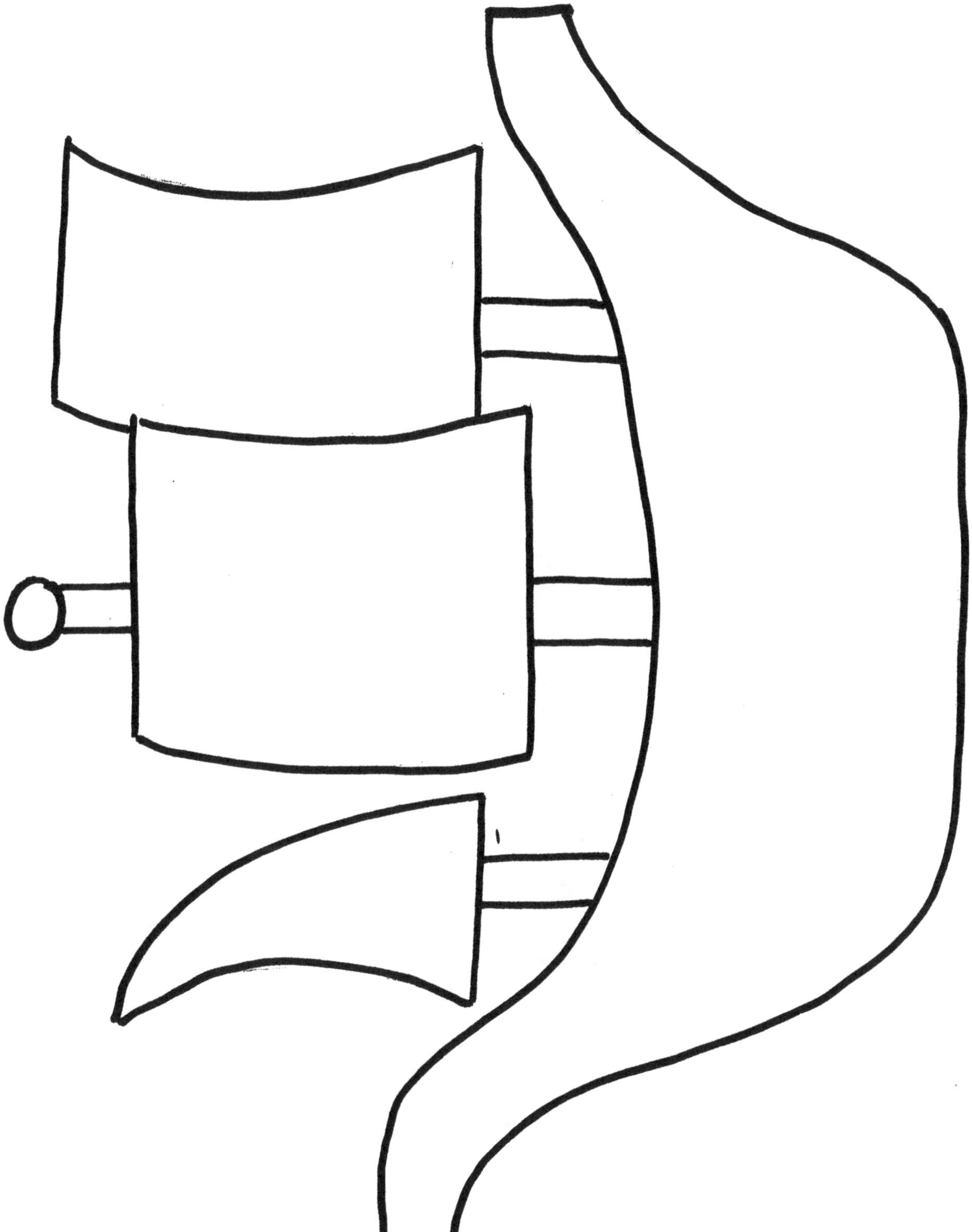

October
Life-in-a-Tree Step Book 1

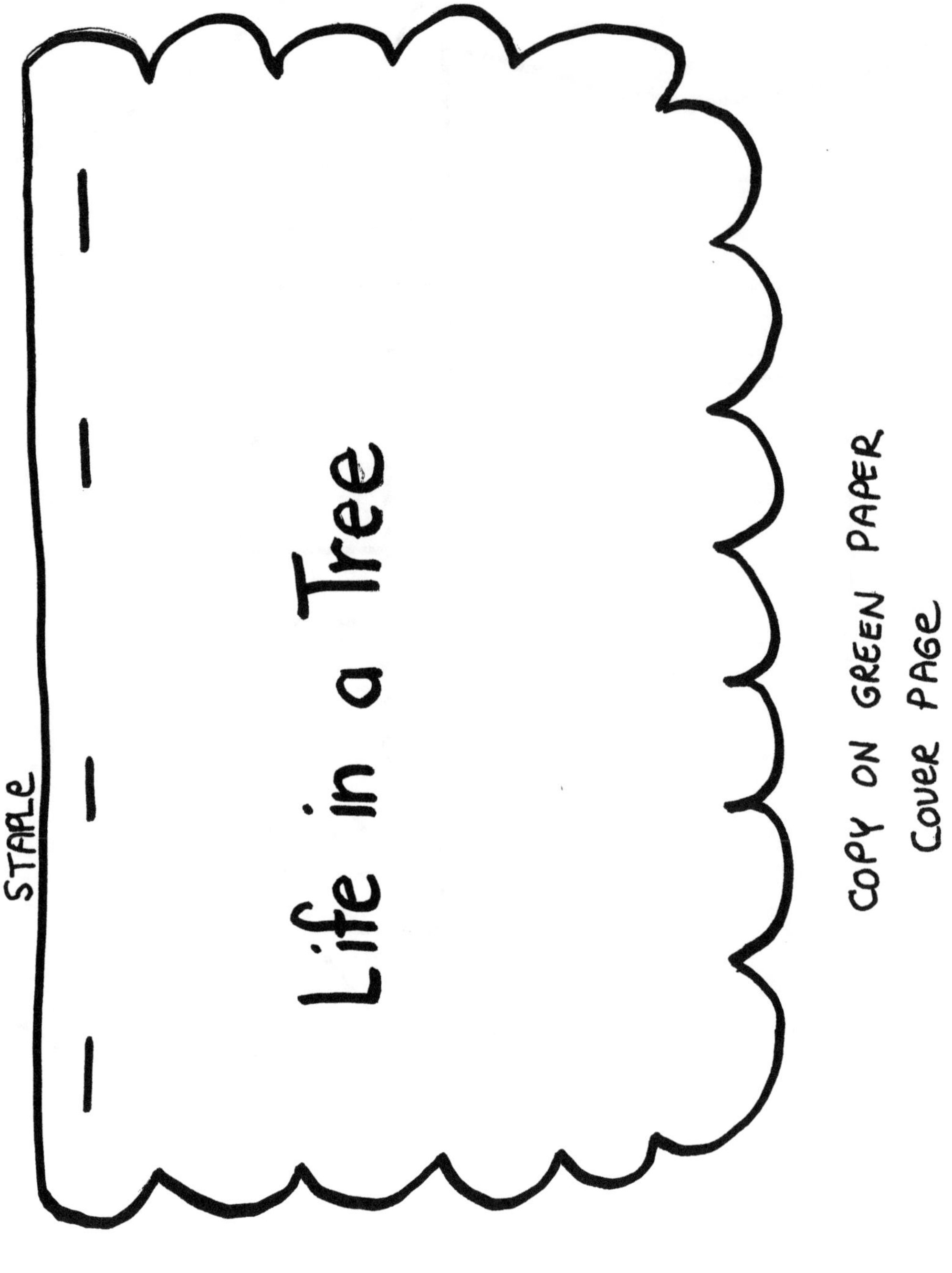

October
Life-in-a-Tree Step Book 2

COPY ON YELLOW PAPER
PAGE ONE

October
Life-in-a-Tree Step Book 3

COPY ON ORANGE PAPER
PAGE TWO

October
Life-in-a-Tree Step Book 4

COPY ON RED PAPER
PAGE 3

October
Life-in-a-Tree Step Book 5

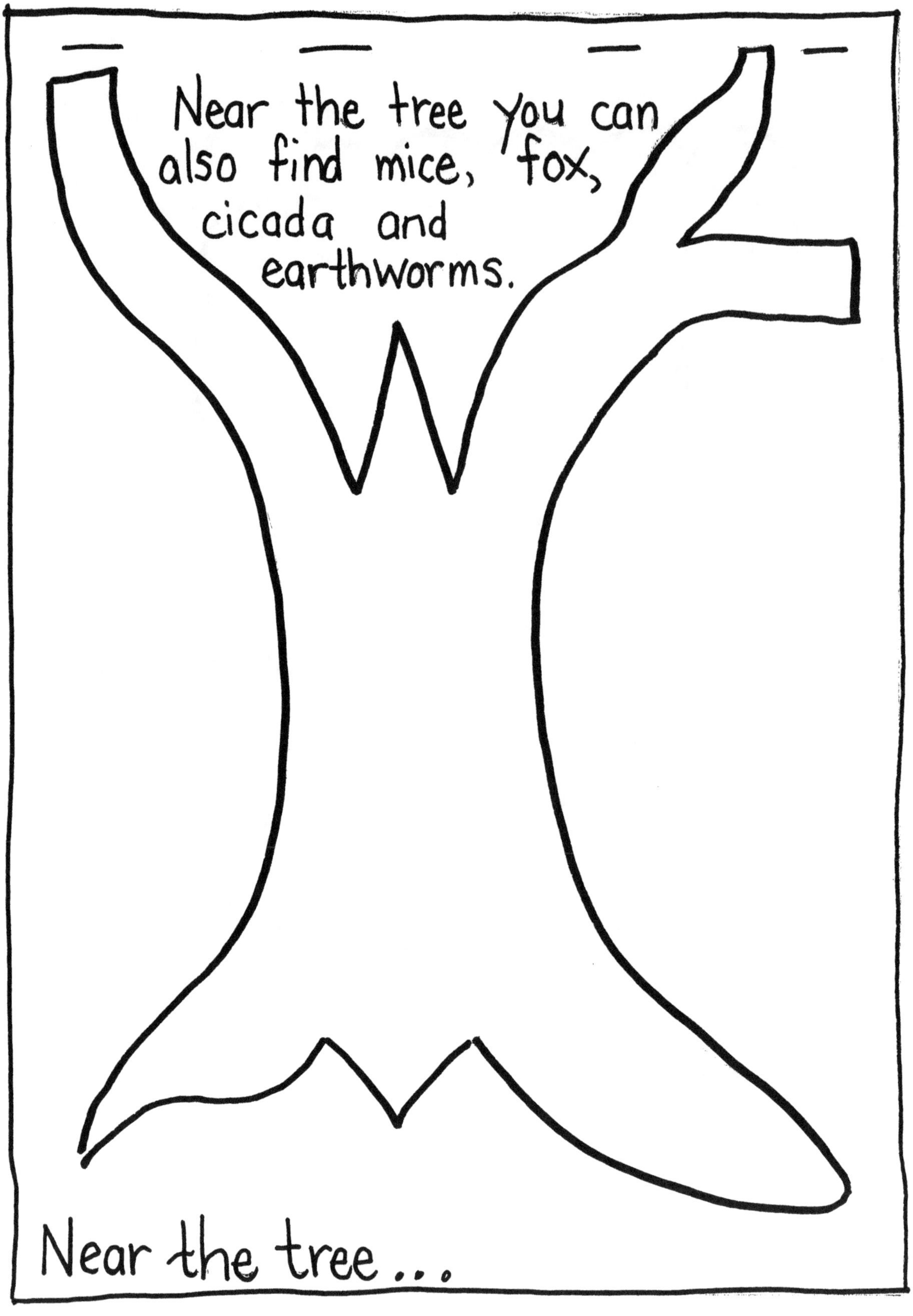

November
Thanksgiving Bag Turkey Head Pattern

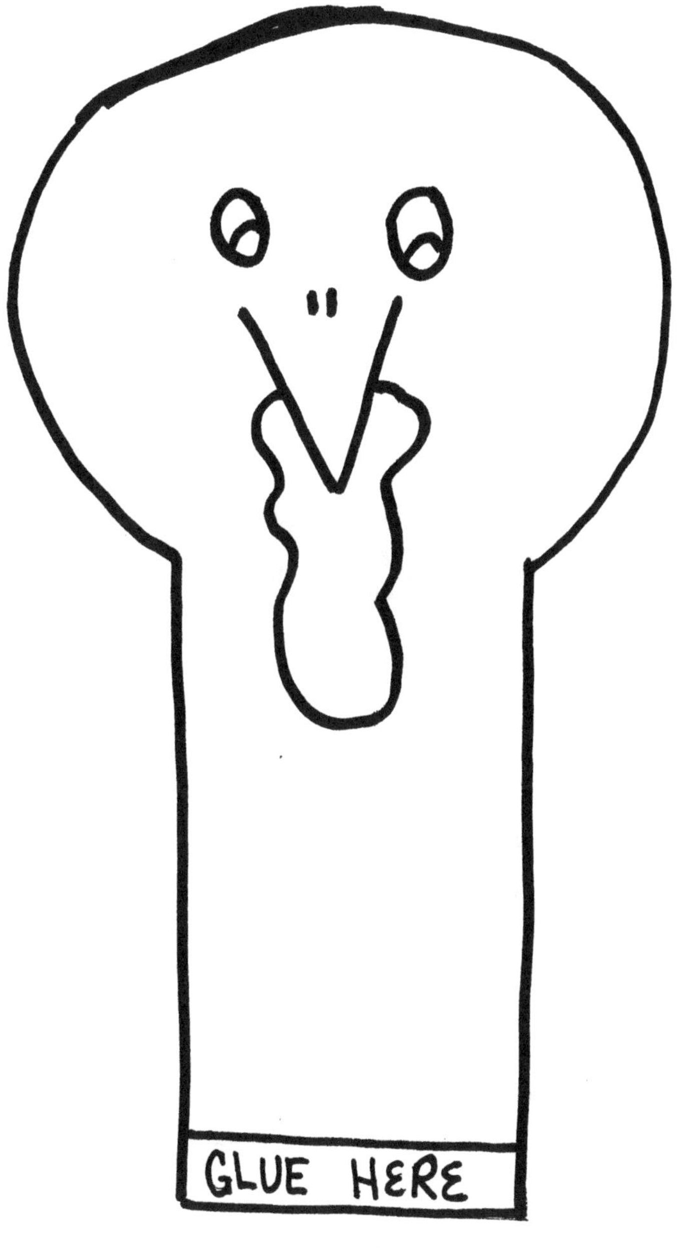

November
Thanksgiving Bag Horn-of-Plenty Pattern

November
Native-American Vest-Pocket Bag Pattern

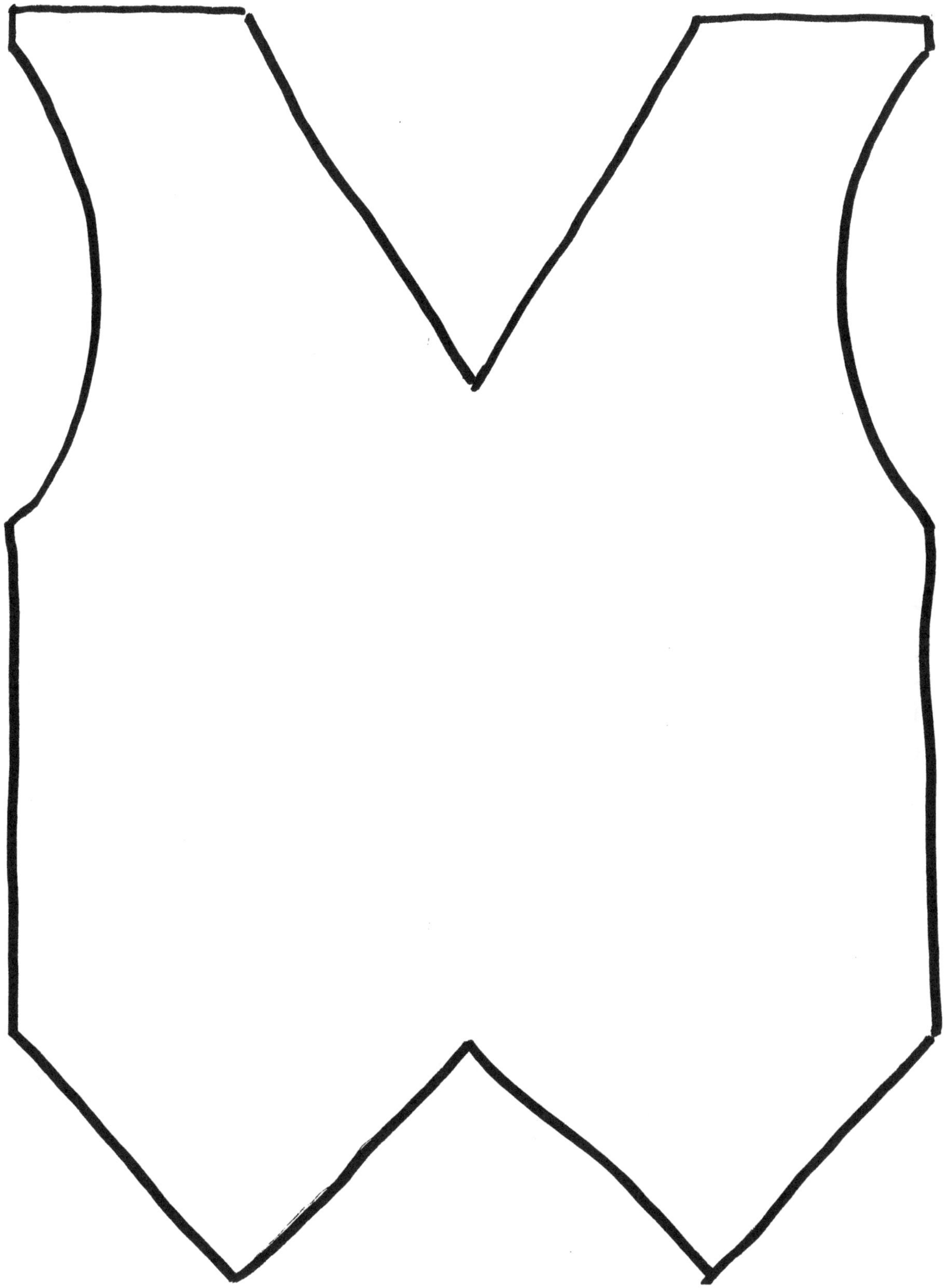

December
Animals-in-Winter Bag Book 1

What Happens to the Animals in Winter?

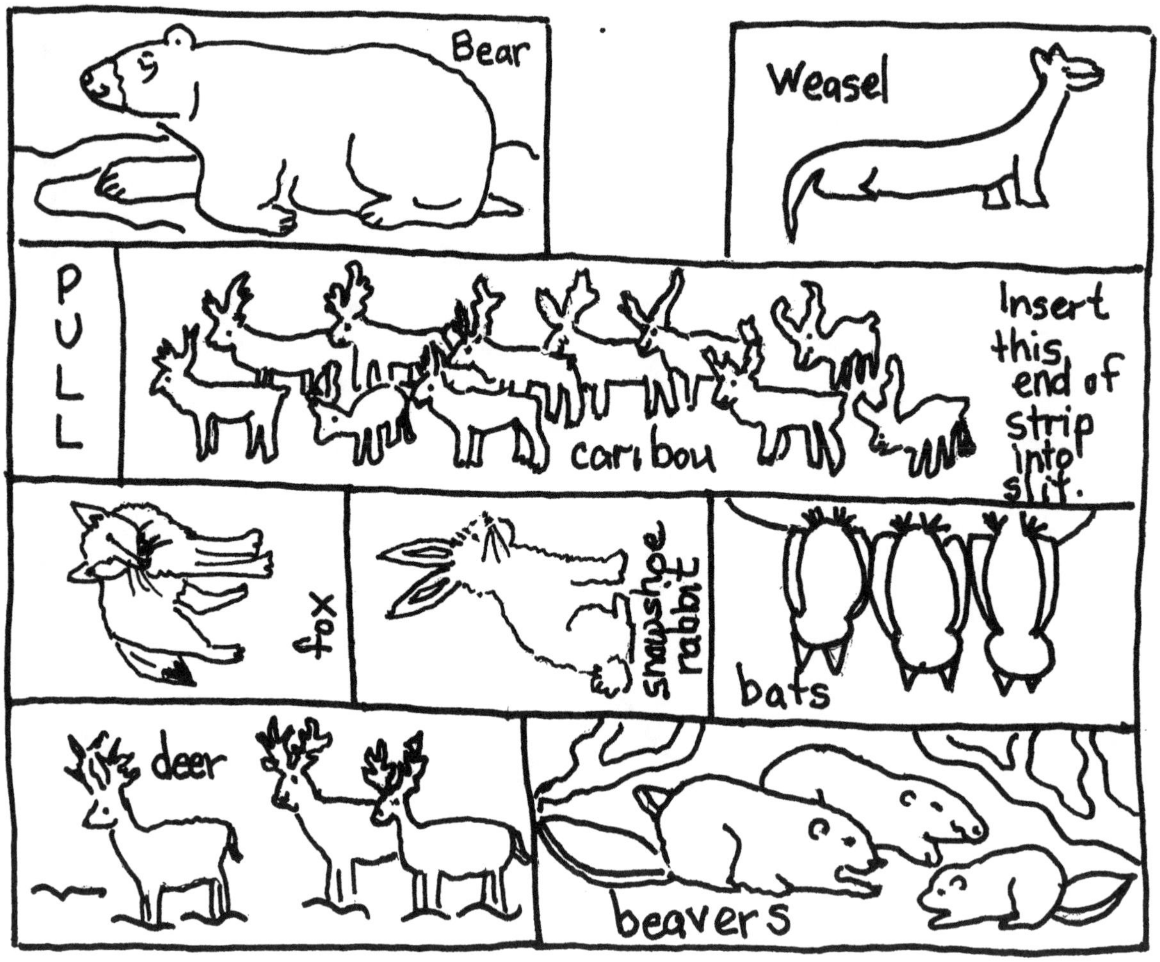

December
Animals-in-Winter Bag Book 2

Some animals hibernate. This means
that they sleep through the winter in
a safe, warm place. Can you identify
the animals that hibernate?

Some animals hibernate. This means

Can you identify the animals that
hibernate?

December
Animals-in-Winter Bag Book 3

Some animals migrate. This means
that the animal leaves its home and
travels to another place. The animal
goes to a warmer place for food.
Which animals choose to migrate?

Some animals migrate. This means

Which animals choose to migrate?

December
Animals-in-Winter Bag Book 4

Some animals are active all winter.
Some active animals change color in
winter to protect them from their
enemies. Which animals are active?

Some animals are active all winter.
These animals must

Which animals are active all winter?

December
Animals-in-Winter Bag Book 5

Some active animals hide in winter.

They hide in their warm homes.

Who would hide in this house?

Some active animals

Who would hide in this house?

January
"I Have a Dream" Bag 1

Martin Luther King
"I have a dream that
my four children will
one day live in a
nation where they will
not be judged by the
color of their skin but
the content of their
character."

My dream for the
future

January
"I Have a Dream" Bag 2

January
"I Have a Dream" Bag 3

January
"I Have a Dream" Bag 4

January
Coin Timeline

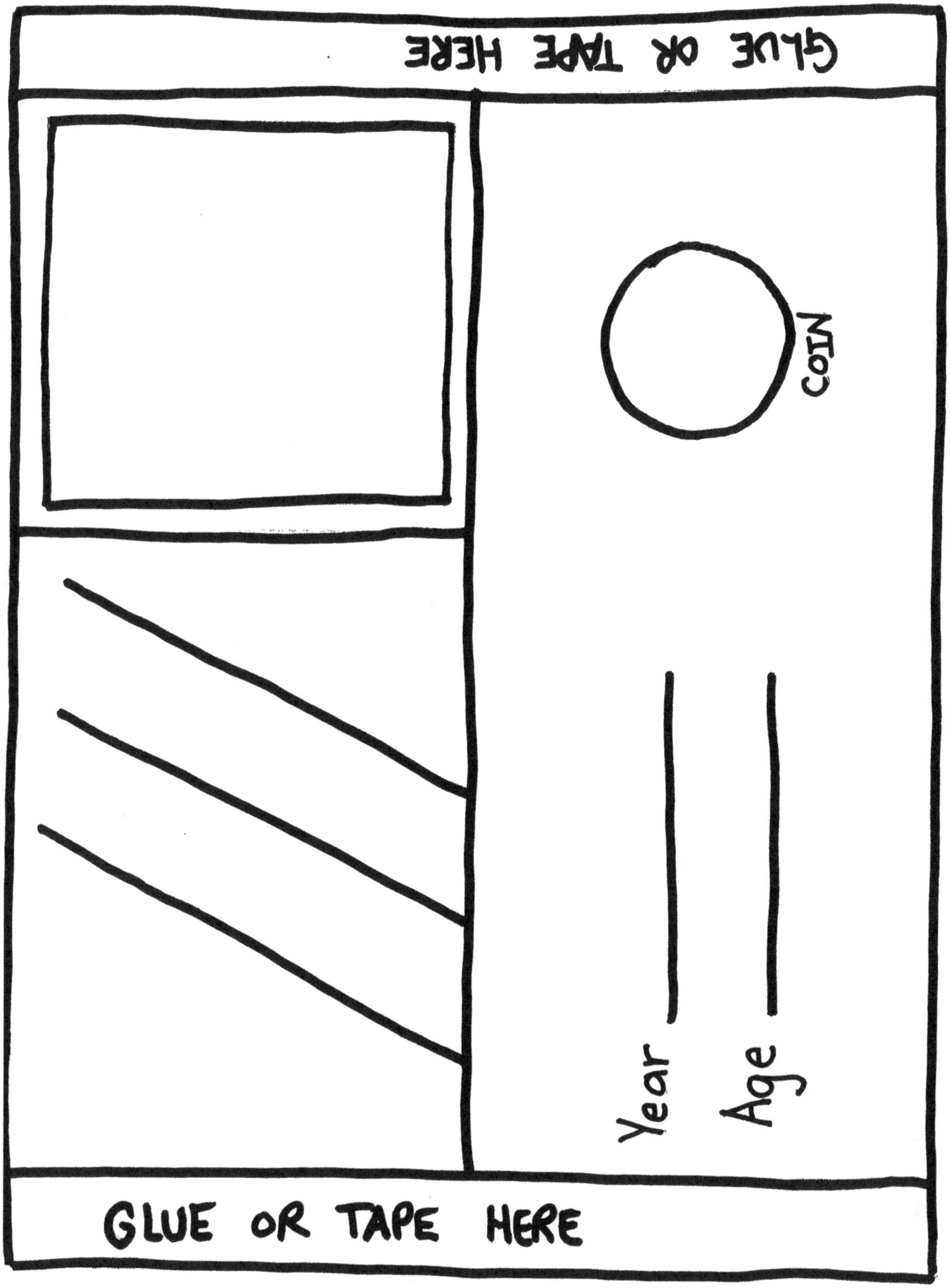

January
My Special Dream

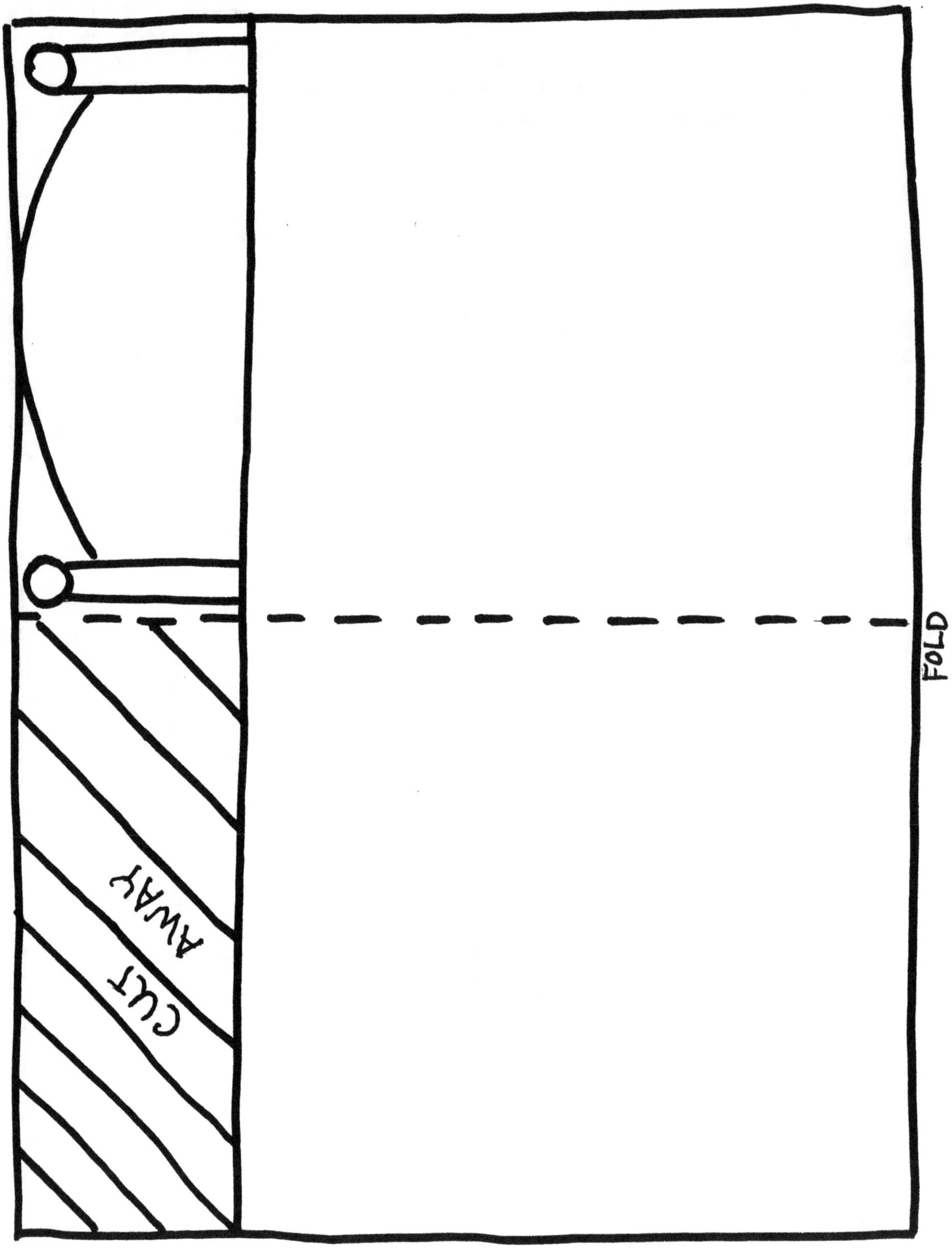

February
Toolbox Tools 1

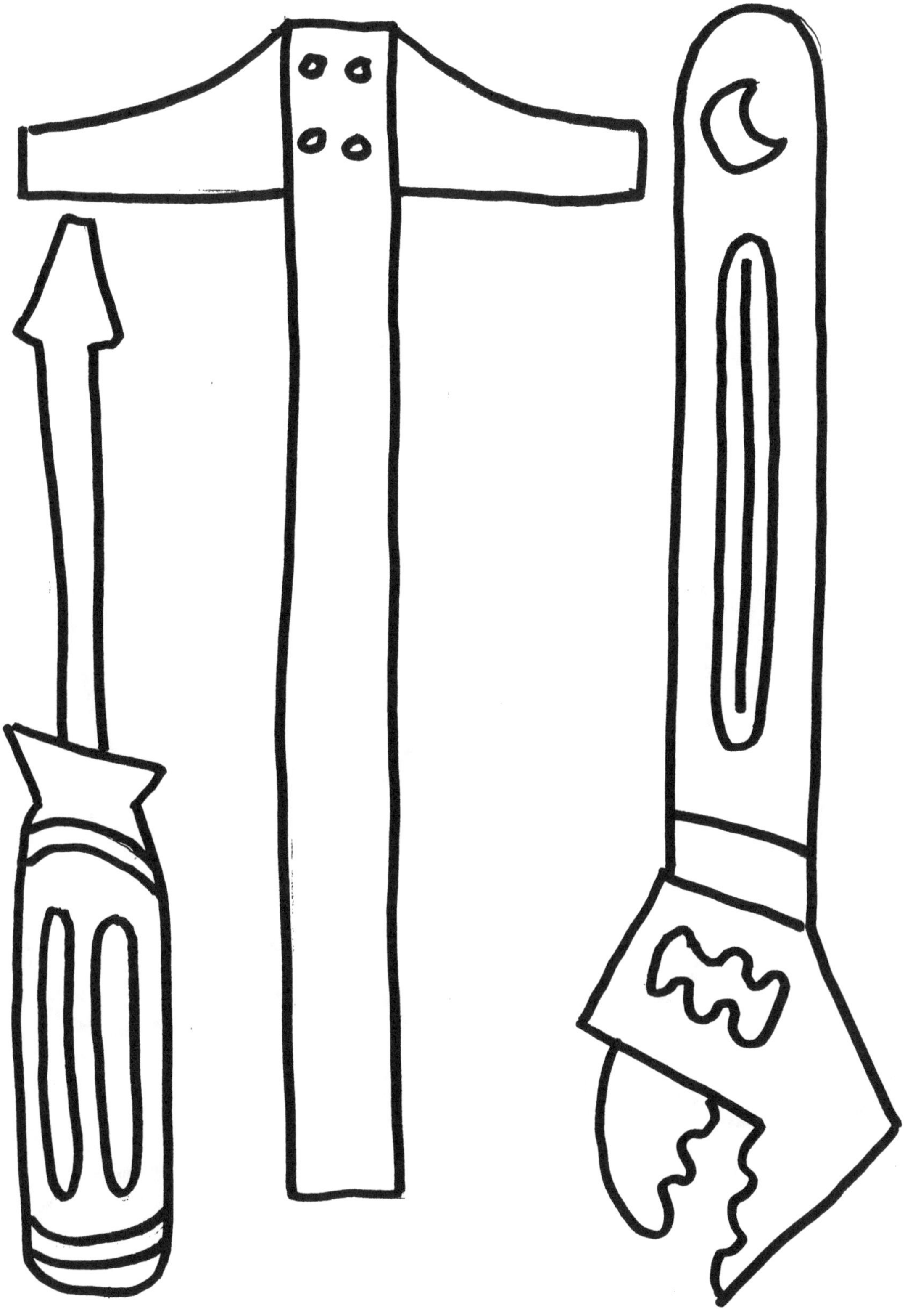

February
Toolbox Tools 2

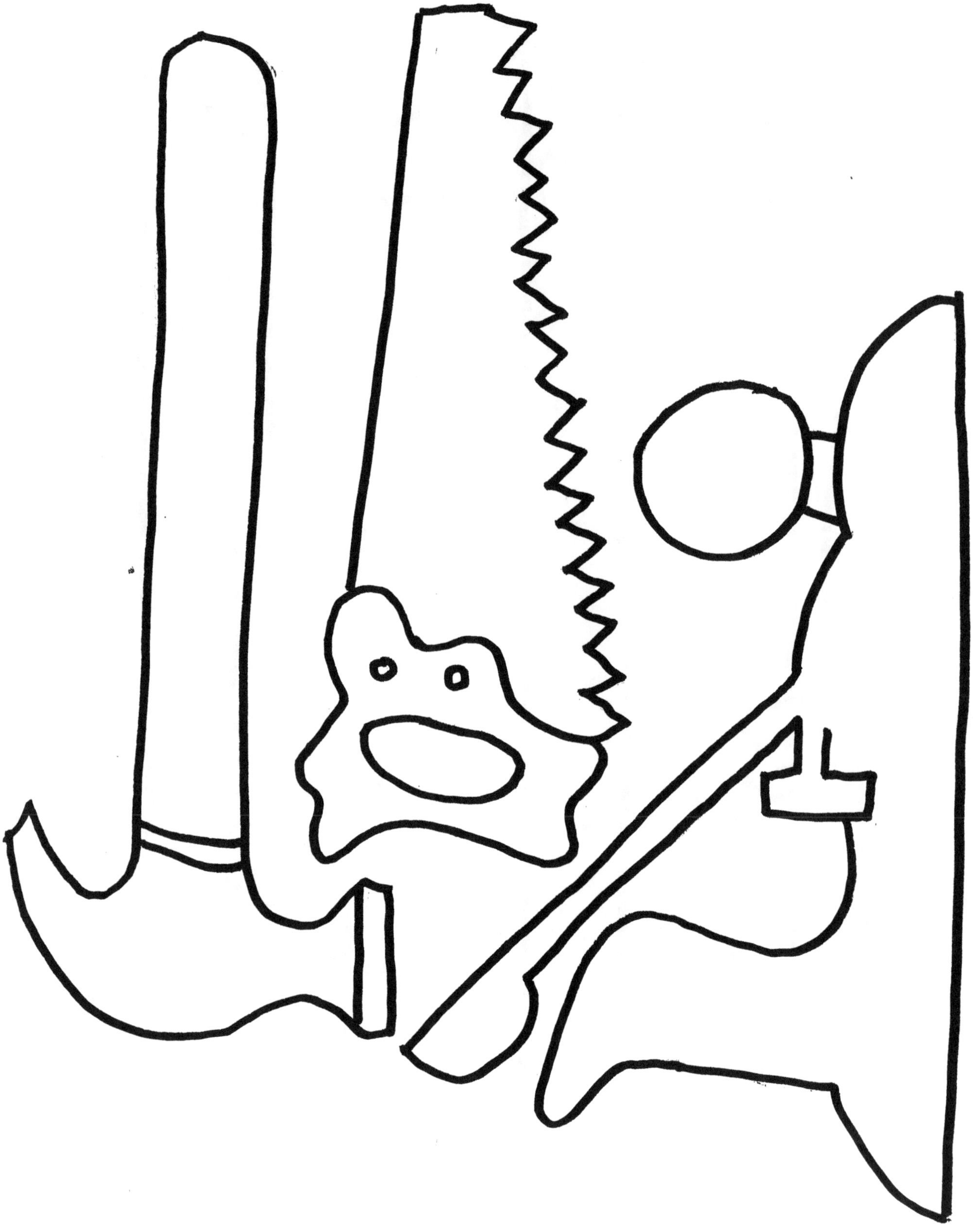

February
Face

February
Career Camera 1

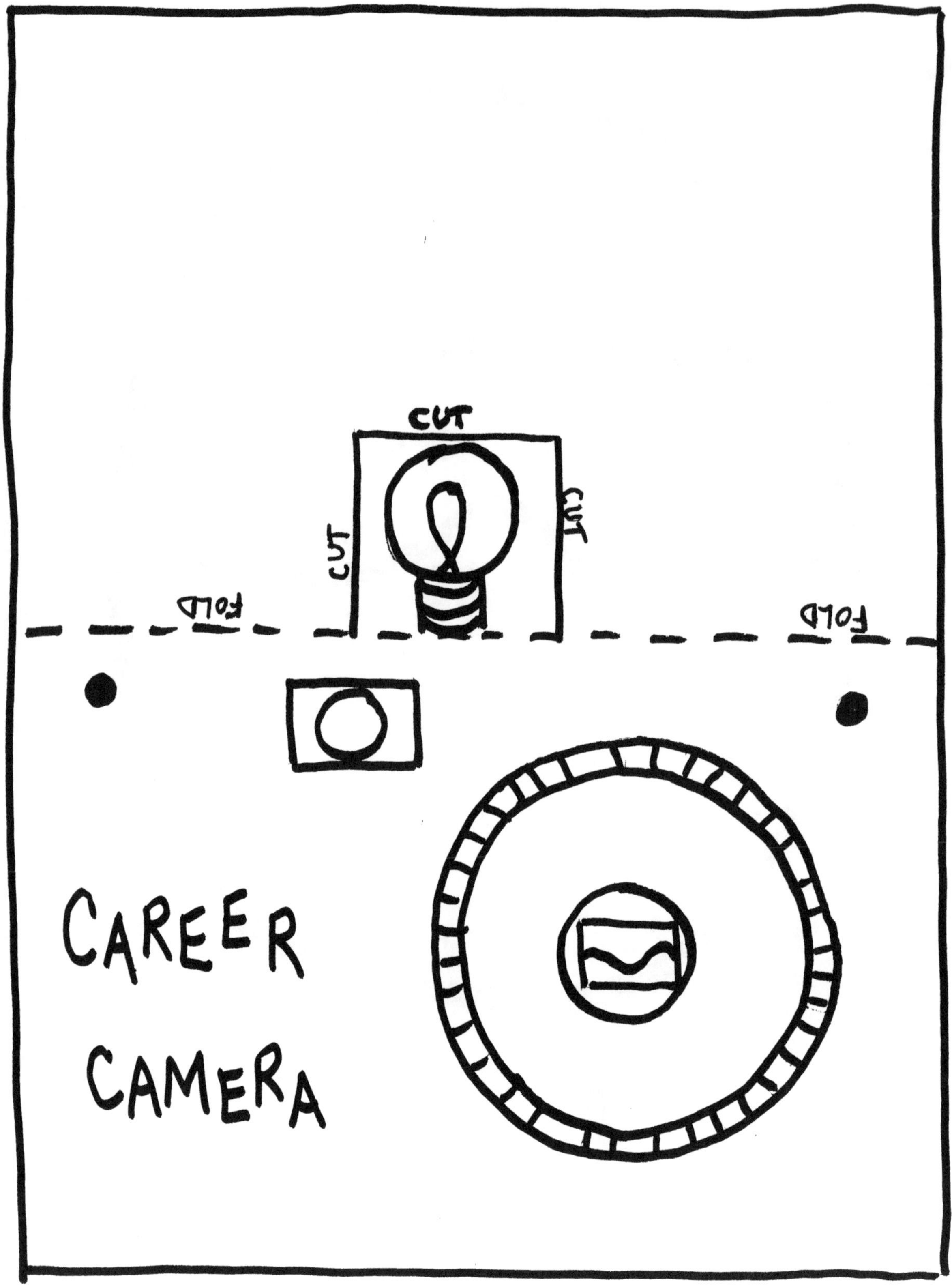

February
Career Camera 2

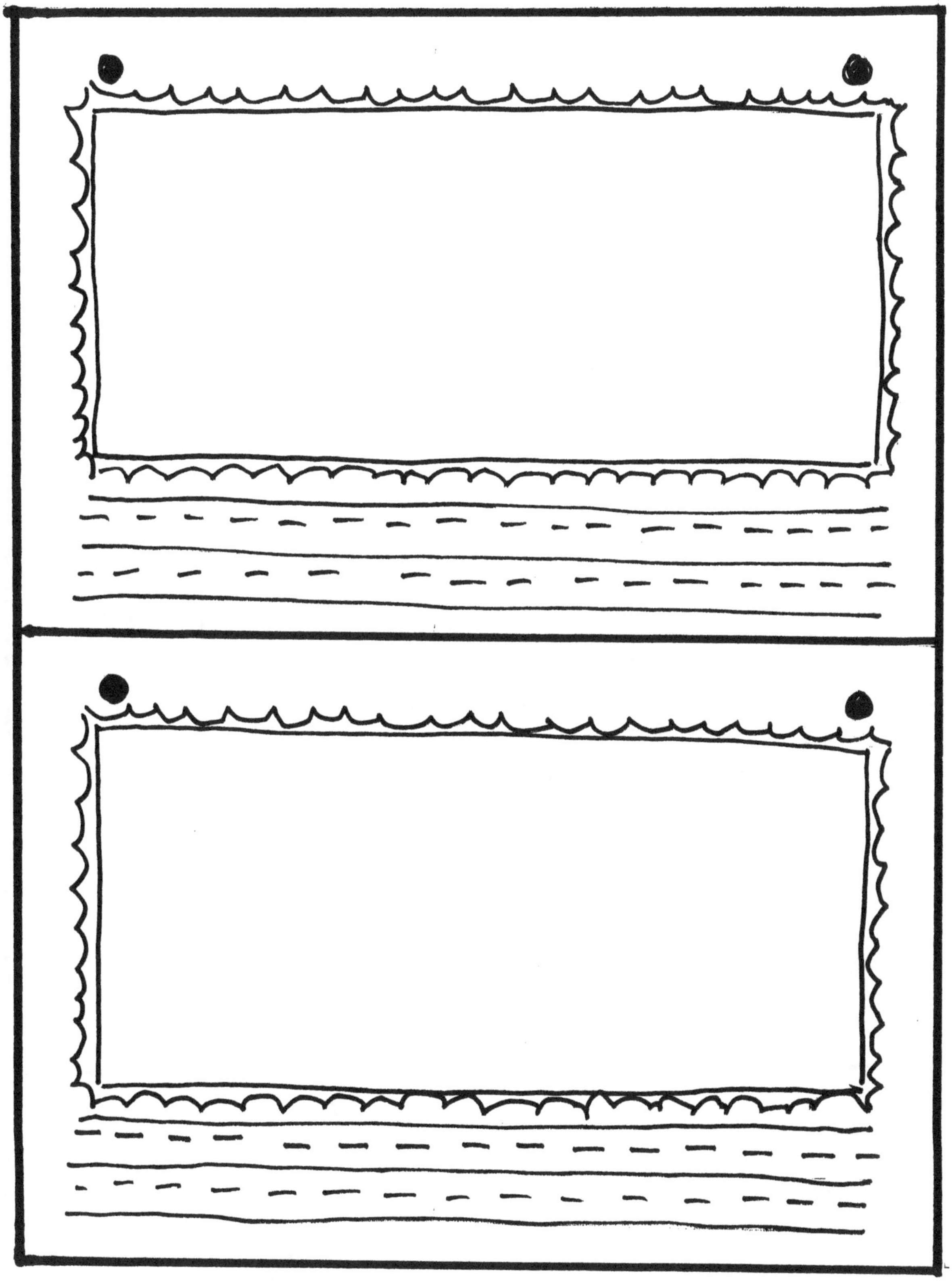

March
Up-in-the-Air Bag Hot-Air Balloon

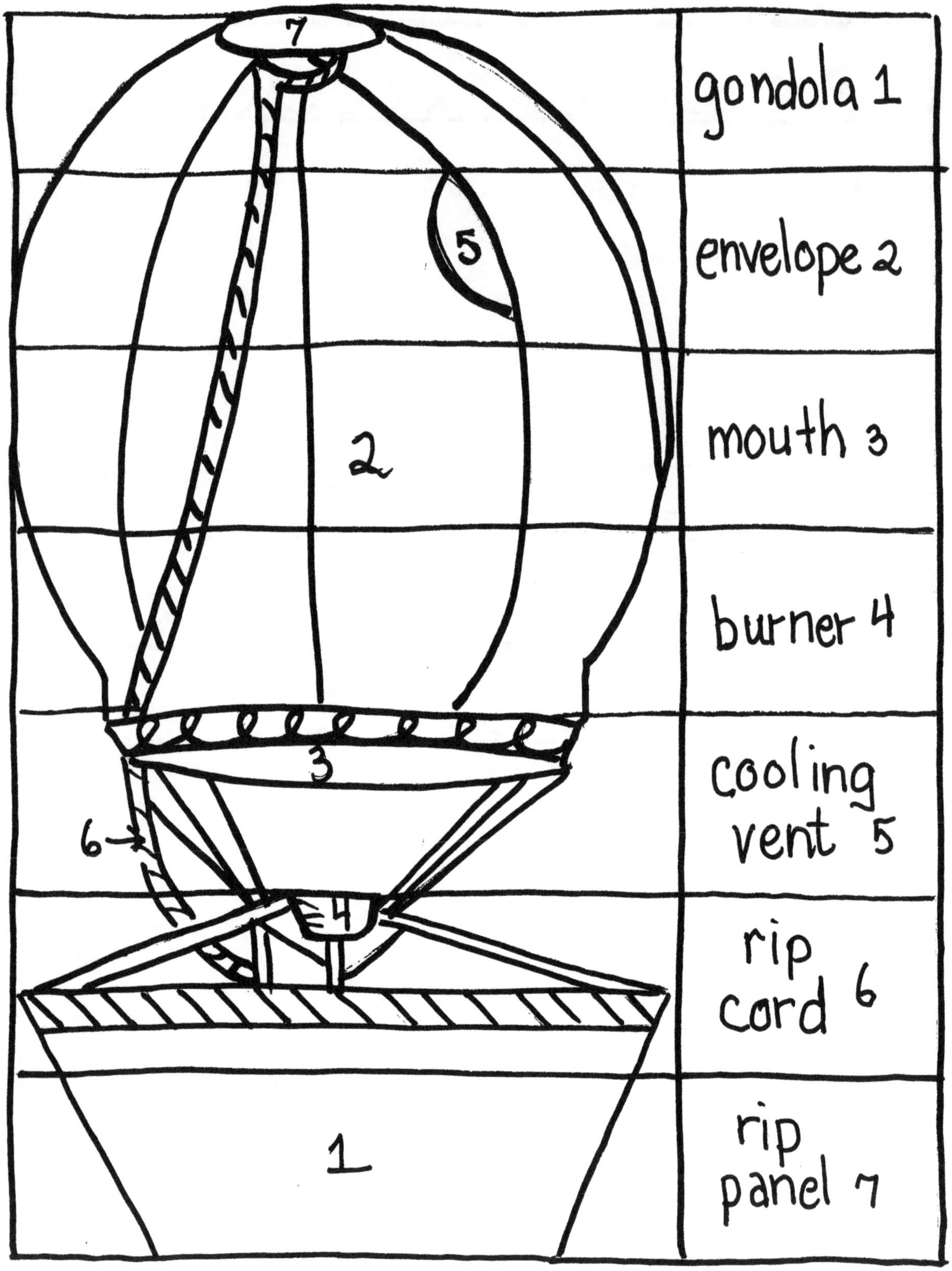

March
Cloud Tissue-Box Windows 1

*CREATE YOUR OWN CLOUDS.

March
Cloud Tissue-Box Windows 2

NIMBOSTRATUS ARE SEEN WITH FOG, RAIN OR SNOW.

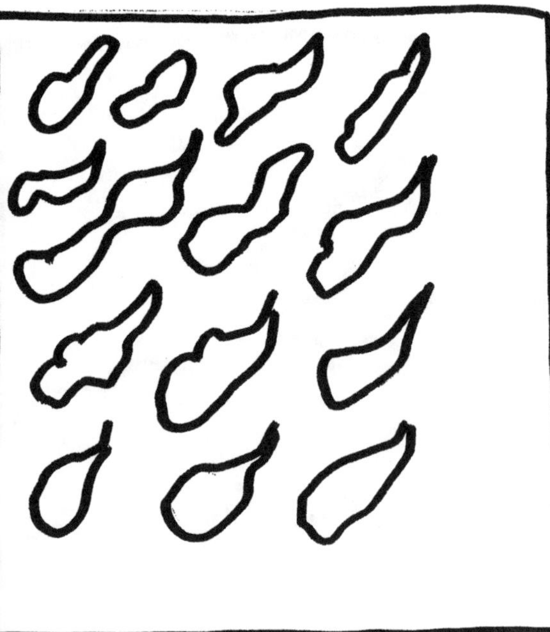

CIRROSTRATUS TELL YOU IT WILL RAIN SOON.

CUMULONIMBUS ARE SEEN WITH RAIN, THUNDER AND LIGHTNING.

CREATE YOUR OWN CLOUDS

March
Up-in-the-Air/Right-on-the-Ground
Airline Ticket 1

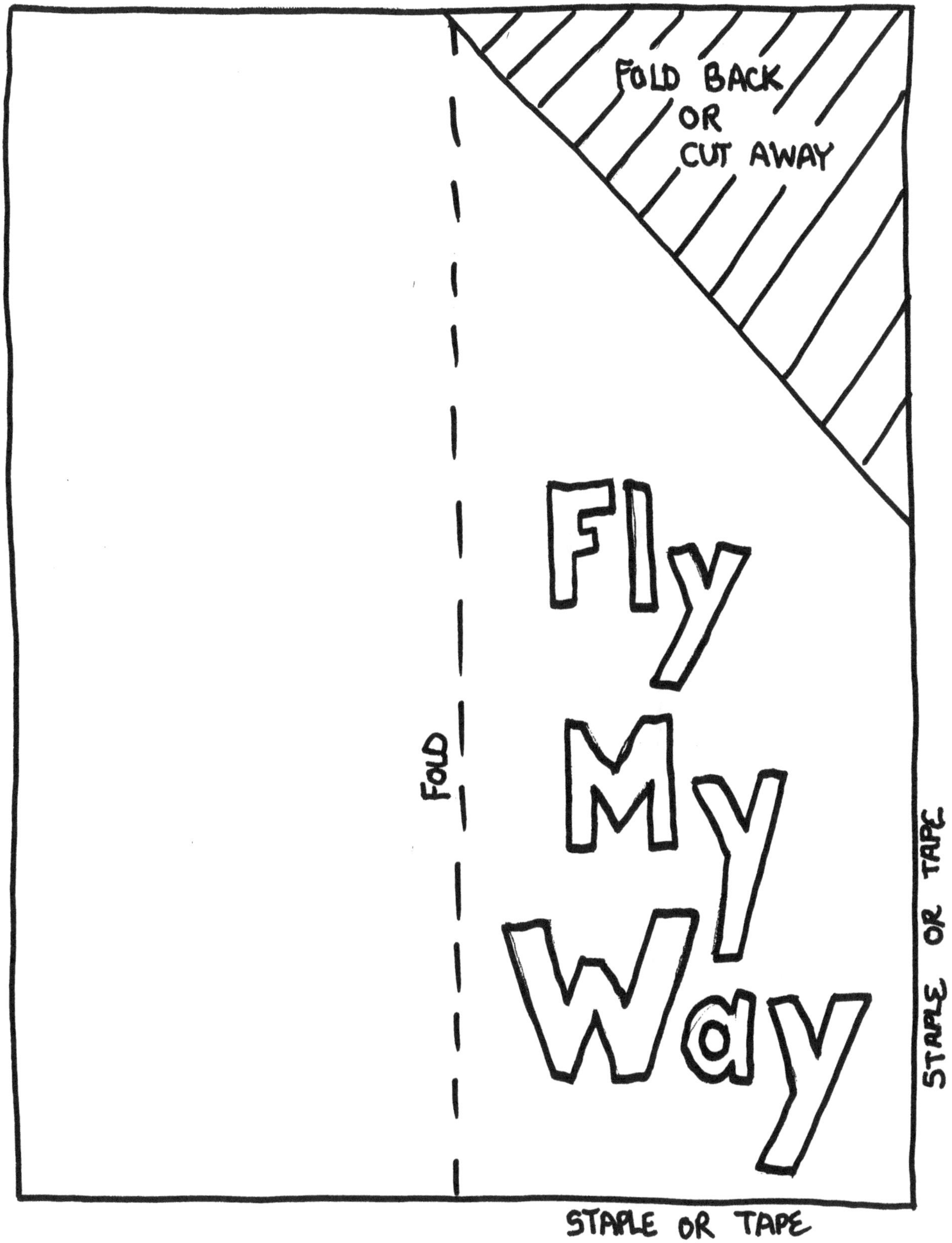

March
Up-in-the-Air/Right-on-the-Ground
Airline Ticket 2

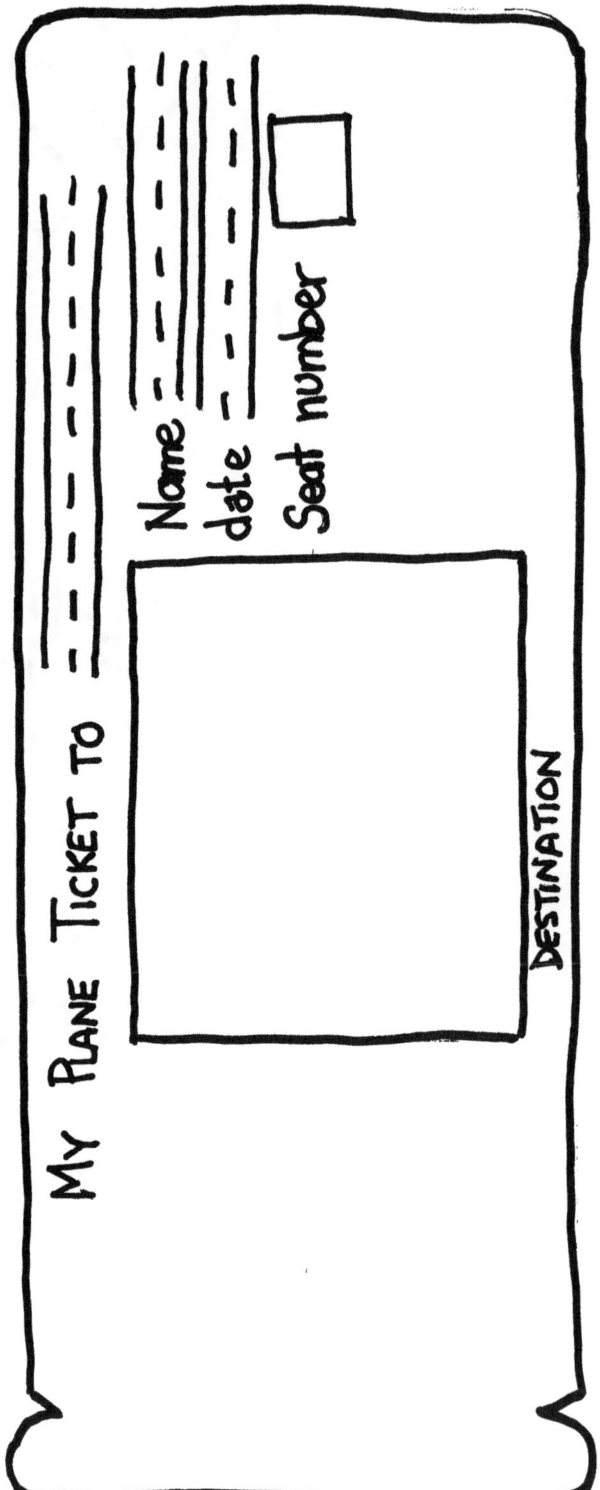

April
Shower Flower Backpack 1

April
Shower Flower Backpack 2

April
Shower Flower Backpack 3

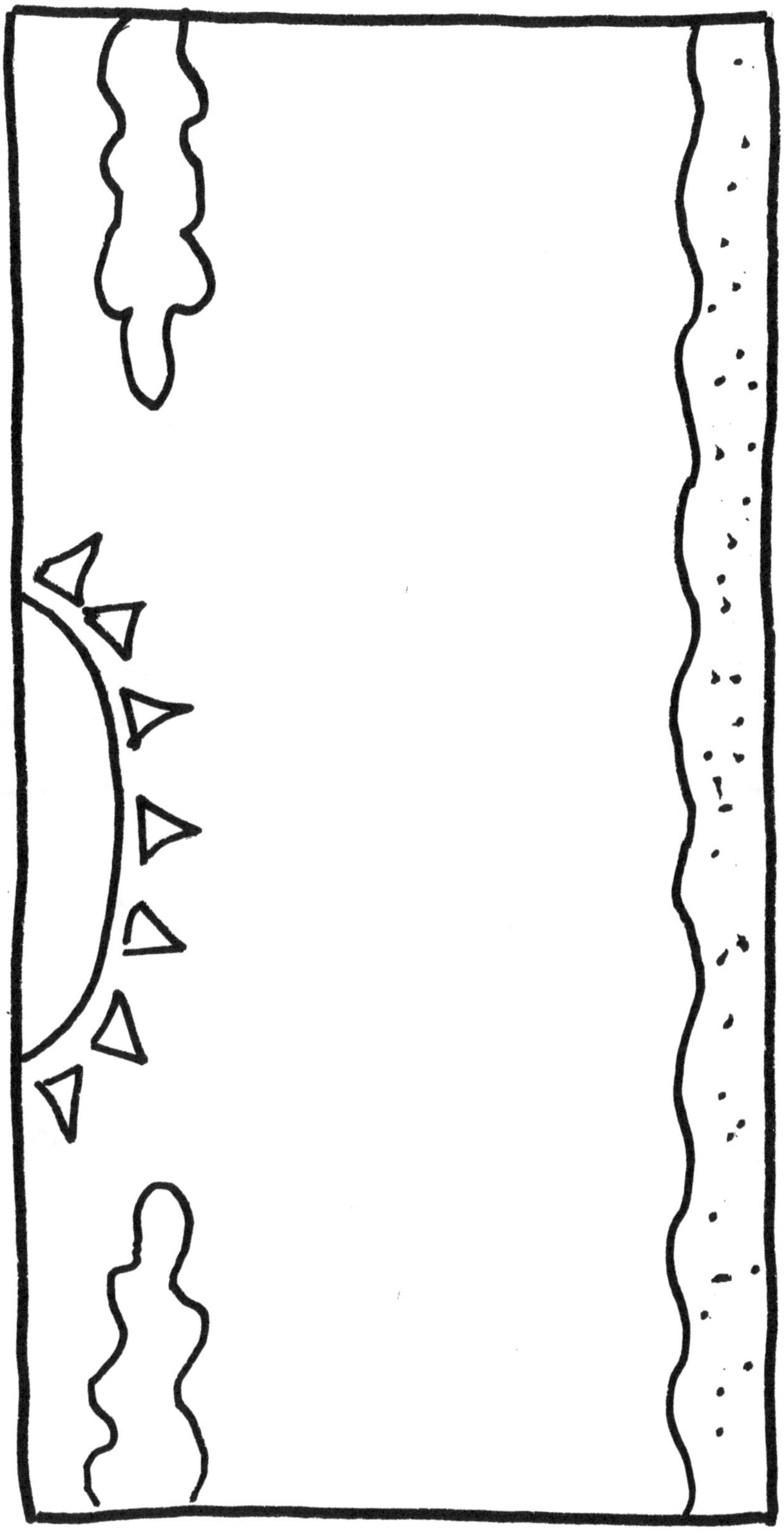

April

Shower Flower Backpack 4

Sun	Land	Water
Clouds	Evaporation	
Precipitation	Condensation	
Rain	Roots	Stem
Seed	Petal	Flower

April
Seed-Packet Book 1

April
Seed-Packet Book 2

About My Plant...

May
Environment Bag 1

What does my Earth have?

My Earth has forests.

My Earth has deserts.

My Earth has rain forests.

My Earth has oceans.

My Earth has Arctic regions.

My Earth has mountains.

May
Environment Bag 2

My Earth has forests, deserts,
rain forests, oceans, Arctic
regions, mountains, and me!

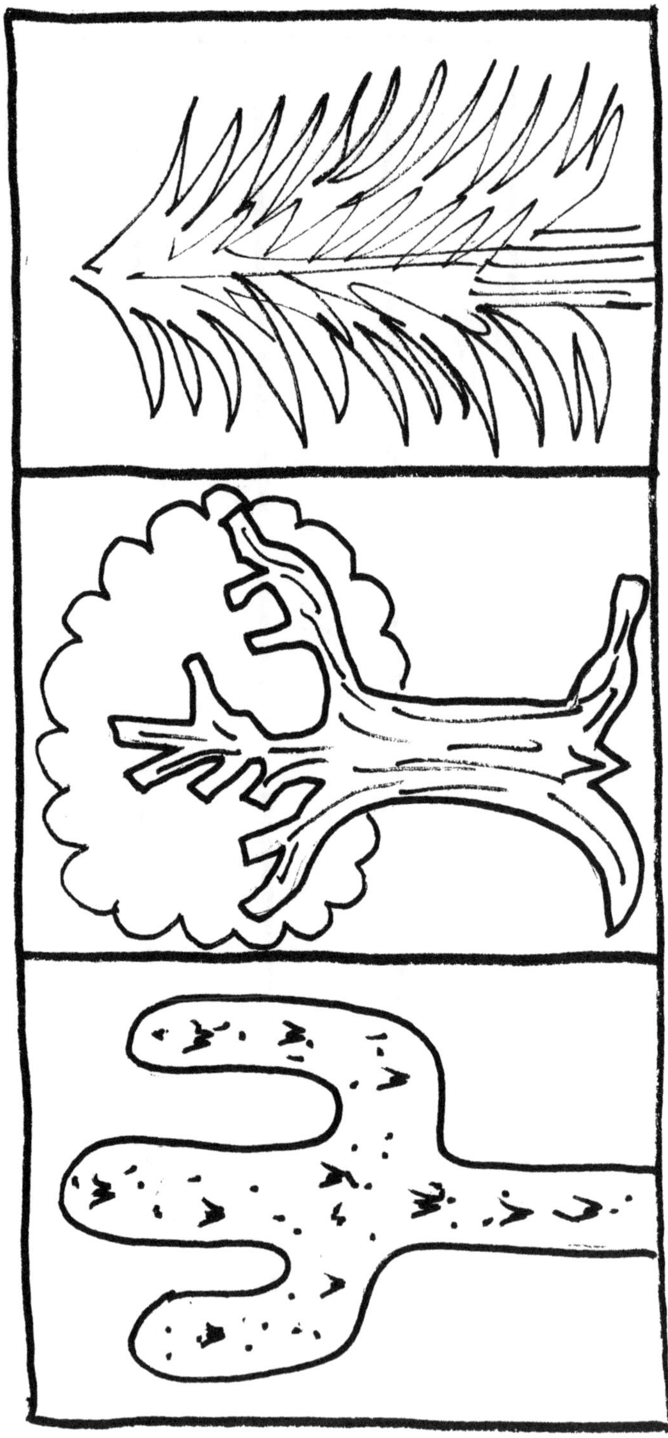

May
Environment Bag 3

May
Environment Bag 4

May
Environment Bag 5

OPTIONAL ENERGY PAGE

May

CD Accordion Book 1

May
CD Accordion Book 2

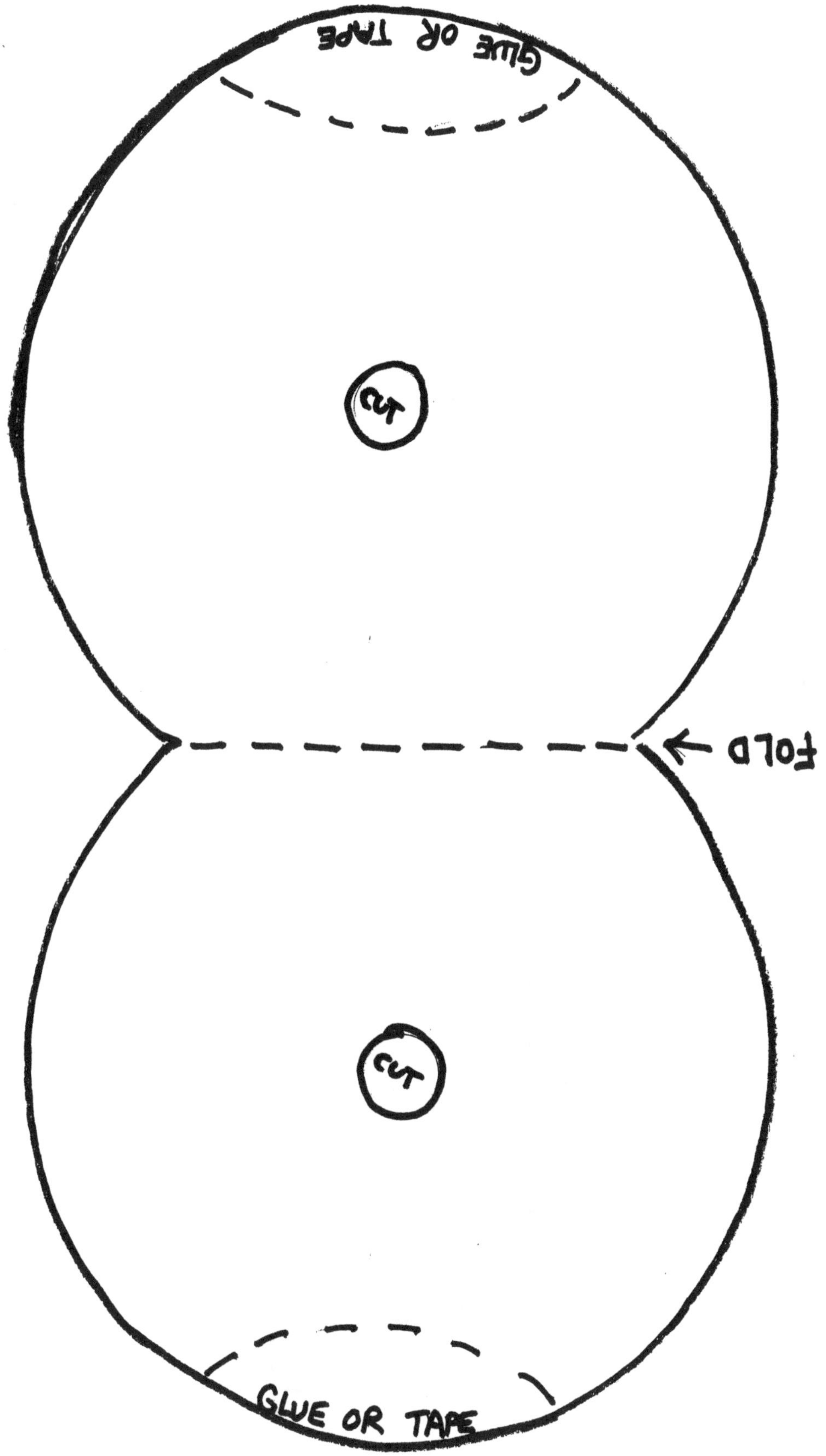

Summer
Palm Tree Bag

Summer Postcard

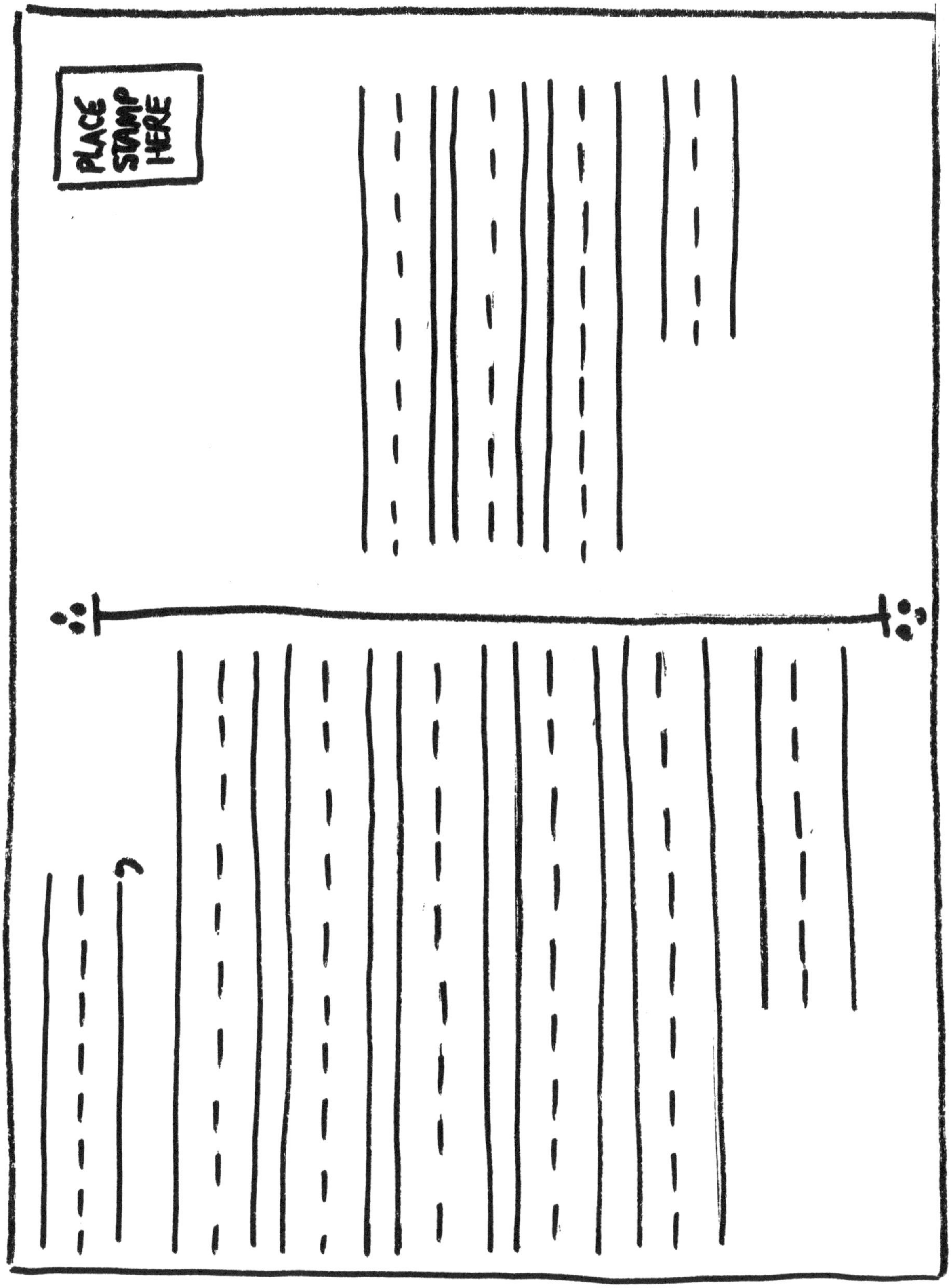